# Serbia

# Serbia

BY
## JoAnn Milivojevic

*Enchantment of the World*
*Second Series*

## Children's Press®

*A Division of Grolier Publishing*

New York   London   Hong Kong   Sydney
Danbury, Connecticut

*Consultant:*   Dr. Tatyana Nestorova, Lecturer, Undergraduate International Studies
Program, The Ohio State Universty

*Please note:* All statistics are as up-to-date as possible at the time of publication.

Visit Children's Press on the Internet: *http://publishing.grolier.com*


Library of Congress Cataloging-in-Publication Data

Milivojevic, JoAnn.
    Serbia / by JoAnn Milivojevic.
        p.      cm. — (Enchantment of the world. Second series)
    Includes bibliographical references and index.
    Summary: An introduction to the geography, history, economy, natural
resources, culture, and people of Serbia, the larger of the
two republics that make up the country of Yugoslavia.
    ISBN 0-516-21196-X
    1. Serbia—Juvenile literature. [1. Serbia.] I. Title. II. Series.
DR1940.M55   1999
949.71—dc21                                                                    98-19256
                                                                                    CIP
                                                                                    AC

## Acknowledgments

I'd like to thank my family and friends who so generously gave of their time. This book would not have been possible without them. Special thanks to Mira Obradovich for her excellent translation services, historical knowledge, and for tirelessly accompanying me on my Serbia travels; to Rev. Father Tom Kazich for information on the Orthodox religion; to Dragan Kecman for his cultural insights and artistic talent; and to my mother, Radmila Milivojevic, who has fostered relationships between me and my relatives in Serbia. This book is dedicated to her and in memory of my father.

# Contents

**Cover photo:**
Sopocani Monastery

The grape harvest

A pine marten

Cyril and Methodius, creators of
the Cyrillic alphabet

# Crossroads

Serbia is a small land that has had significant impact upon world history and politics. As you explore Serbia, you will discover a treasure chest filled with art, culture, and tradition. It has ancient monasteries, intricate mosaics, epic poems, and a long list of accomplished artists and scholars. From Ivo Andrić, winner of the 1961 Nobel Prize for literature, to Nikola Tesla, the electrical engineer who invented alternating current (AC), Serbia's writers, scientists, scholars, and athletes have made important contributions.

The monastery of Peć

*Opposite:* **Serbian countryside in autumn**

**Many monasteries in Serbia are decorated with frescoes.**

S ERBIA IS A CROSSROADS WHERE FOR centuries people from different backgrounds have met. Some stayed, adding their own cultural flavor to the Serbian mix. The combination of cultures can be seen in Islamic mosques built alongside Orthodox churches, in ancient fresco paintings and modern art, and in Turkish coffee and *šlivovitz,* a Serbian brandy.

Serbia has crowded modern cities and quiet villages. Serbian people pick medicinal herbs for natural healing; wash down fast foods with mineral water; and have their own version of rock and roll music—often a blend of ethnic and American sounds.

### The Balkans

From the fifteenth to the nineteenth centuries, the Ottoman Empire (also known as the Turkish Empire) ruled over an area in the southeast corner of Europe that became known as the Balkans. Today, the term is used to define a region of republics and countries that includes Slovenia, Croatia, Bosnia and Herzegovina, Macedonia, Yugoslavia

Geopolitical map of Serbia

(which includes Serbia and Montenegro), Albania, Greece, Romania, Bulgaria, and Turkey.

Serbia has been called the heart of the Balkans. The name *Balkan* refers to a mountain range that runs through the area. In fact, the word *Balkan* means "mountain" in Turkish. But Balkan is not only a geographical reference, it also refers to the spirit of the people who live there. It is a freedom-loving and passion-filled way of life that has been captured in music, literature, and painting.

### Rivers Cross, Mountains Meet, Nations Merge

If you've done any cloud-watching, you know that the fluffy white masses can look like familiar shapes. Countries can also resemble objects. Italy, for example, looks like a boot, with its heel near southern Yugoslavia.

**A Belgrade street scene**

As you look at the map of Serbia, notice that the northern part looks like the head of a lion. Its nose touches the borders of Hungary and Croatia. The Danube River curling in toward Novi Sad is the animal's open mouth. Under its chin is the border of Bosnia and Herzegovina, and its extended front legs are in Montenegro. Belgrade—where the lion's mane would be—is the capital city of Serbia and Yugoslavia.

**A discarded canon overlooks an Orthodox church and a mosque in Prizren, Kosovo**

In 1918, several regions—Slovenia, Croatia, Bosnia and Herzegovina, Serbia, Macedonia, and Montenegro—joined together to form the Kingdom of the Serbs, Croats, and Slovenes. The kingdom was renamed Yugoslavia in 1929. In the early 1990s, this union fell apart when several republics declared independence and broke away from Yugoslavia.

Today, the Federal Republic of Yugoslavia (FRY) consists of Serbia and Montenegro. Montenegro is a rocky and dry expanse of land that touches the Adriatic Sea north of Albania. Montenegrin men sometimes call themselves "tall" Serbs. The two republics share a common heritage, but if you ever visit them, you'll see for yourself that Montenegrins tend to be taller. They seem as rugged as the land they live on.

Serbia forms a natural gateway between several countries in southern Europe. Its central location has been a boon to

Serbia's economy and heritage. Serbia was—and still is—a religious crossroads, a place where many beliefs mix and mingle. Today, the people of Serbia follow a number of religions including Christianity, Judaism, and Islam.

The bad side of living in a crossroads is that it can be a meeting place for conflict. As we approach the next millennium, the people of Serbia find themselves again in the middle of things, not only physically but also emotionally. Families were torn apart by the civil war of the early 1990s and the collapse of the economy, which left many people without money and without jobs. But the people of Serbia have always been strong-willed and determined. Slowly, life is rebuilding. The government and the economy are changing. People are developing new businesses and building hope for the future. But no matter which way the political winds blow, Serbia's rich farmland will always be able to feed the people. In that respect, Serbia is fortunate.

**Farmers east of Belgrade driving a horse and wagon**

# From the Mountains to the Valleys

"Over the river and through the woods" is a good way to describe a journey around Serbia. It is a land of rushing rivers and crystal-clear lakes, dense forests and damp caves, and mountains rich in minerals. Serbia is a small land. At 34,115 square miles (88,358 sq km), it is about the size of the U.S. state of Maine.

# F
## Mountains

LAT PLAINS STRETCH ACROSS THE northernmost region of Serbia. The rest of the country is covered with rolling hills, green valleys, and high mountains. The Dinaric Alps are on the west, the Albanian Alps and the Šar Mountains rise in the southwest, and the Balkan Mountains are to the east. The North Albanian Alps in southern Serbia have the nation's highest peaks, rising almost 9,000 feet (2,743 m).

Many of Serbia's mountains have become popular tourist centers, including Kopaonik, Tara, and Zlatibor. The mountainsides are covered with deciduous and evergreen forests, wildflower meadows, and grassy pastures. People flock to these areas all year round to ski, fish, hike, and ride horses.

Hikers in a forest in eastern Serbia

*Opposite:* **A mountain stream near Peć**

## A Land of Threes

From top to bottom, Serbia can be divided into three geographical regions. In the north is the province of Vojvodina (VOY-voh-dee-na), a large area of fertile plains drained by the Danube, Sava, and Tisa Rivers. Central Serbia is a hilly region with the highest population. In the south is the province of Kosovo, a drier and more rocky mountainous region.

The name Vojvodina comes from the Serbian word *vojvoda*, which means "chieftain." The area is an extension of the Great Hungarian Plain. Millions of years ago, this region was under the sea. Earthquakes eventually pushed the land up out of the water. The province has three distinct sections: Srem, immediately north of the city of Belgrade; Bačka (northwest); and Banat (northeast).

### Geographical Features

**Area:** 34,115 square miles (88,358 sq km)
**Largest City:** Belgrade (pop. 1,602,226)
**Highest Mountain Peak:** Daravica, 8,714 feet (2,656 m)
**Longest Navigable River:** The Danube travels for 365 miles (588 km) through Serbia.
**Average Temperatures:** 70°F (21°C) in July;
32°F (0°C) in January
**Average Annual Rainfall:** 25–35 inches (64–89 cm)

### Golija Children's Camp

Throughout the year, Serbian schoolchildren spend two weeks at the Golija Children's Camp in Zlatibor. In addition to their regular subjects, they study geography and ecology in a glorious natural setting.

*Opposite:* **Farmland in Vojvodina**

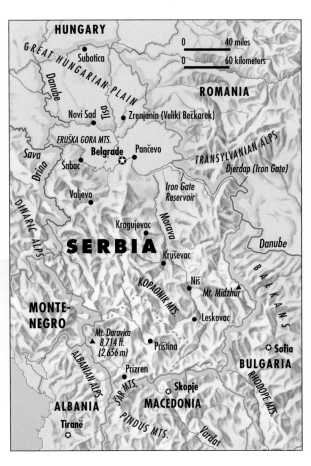

## The Fragrant Linden

You'd have to tip your head way back to see the top of some linden trees because they grow as high as 80 feet (24 m). Walk underneath a linden tree in spring and enjoy the sweet scent of its small white flowers. Bees make honey from the flowers, and people put the blossoms to good use too. They are dried to make a medicinal tea and a special hair rinse. The tea is said to be good for relieving colds; the hair rinse brings out golden highlights.

## Srem

Unlike most of Vojvodina, parts of Srem have gentle rolling hills including a low mountain range called Fruška Gora (FRU-shka Gohr-rah), which means "mountain of fruits." These mountains run between the marshy valleys of the Danube and Sava Rivers. The hills rise to about 1,772 feet (540 m). Much of the area is now a national park protected by the government. The valleys are covered with meadows and grain fields, vineyards, and orchards. Higher areas are capped by dense deciduous forests. The greatest concentration of linden trees in Europe is in this region, and about 700 species of medicinal herbs are found here.

A famous local wine called *fruškogorski biser* is made in this region. Some wine and fruit products are exported, but many families make them for their own use. Farms and vineyards here have been passed down from generation to generation. In Fruška Gora, it is not unusual for a family history to go back 300 years. In addition to grapes for wine, fruits such as plums, pears, and apples are eaten fresh or made into delicious jams.

The Fruška Gora mountain range creates a natural fortress overlooking the plains of the Sava and Danube Rivers. The views from the top of Fruška Gora make it a lovely place to live. The Serbian Orthodox Church recognized this hundreds of years ago and built sixteen monasteries in the area, some dating back to the thirteenth century. Around these monasteries, many villages began to form.

In the late 1300s, Ottoman Turks invaded southern Serbia and many people fled to Fruška Gora. Some people were forced out of their homes. Others hoped to escape slavery under Turkish rulers. In those days, churches were educational and cultural centers as well as religious institutions. The monks were well educated, and teaching was part of their monastery work. Painting and literature flourished in these schools.

Fruška Gora is only an hour or so outside the city of Belgrade. Many city dwellers spend weekends in white stucco cottages on the hillsides. The fresh air and the forest greenery are a welcome relief from the gray, concrete city.

Harvesting grapes at a vineyard

## Krušedol Monastery

Krušedol Monastery is the largest building in Fruška Gora and the most important. It was erected in 1509 in the Serbian-Byzantine style. The interior walls are lined with frescoes, and Krušedol holds the tombs of Serbian royalty, including Prince Milan Obrenović, who died in 1901. The peaceful atmosphere gives visitors a refreshing sense of calm.

**More than 200 species of birds call the Obed Marsh home.**

Srem also is home to the vast Obed Marsh. Created by the Sava and Danube Rivers, it is home to more than 200 species of birds and many exotic marsh flowers. The marsh has few trees, but a large variety of grasses flourish there, including cattails and rushes—grasses with a hollow stem. Birds love the marshy wetlands, where they can find all they need to eat and drink. It's a good place to build a nest, too. In marshes, you'll also find frogs and many water bugs—including the kind that seem to skate on top of the water.

## Bačka

The flat and fertile region know as Bačka (BOTCH-ka) is the agricultural heart of Serbia. Here, farmers grow corn, maize, wheat, barley, and other crops. From above, it looks like a patchwork quilt. The crops are planted in neat squares of green, yellow, and brown. Subotica (SUE-bow-tee-tza), the northernmost city in Serbia, is the market center of Bačka.

Throughout the year, tall mounds of hay dot Bačka's landscape. Each haystack takes two people a couple of days to build. The hay is placed around a wooden post and then stomped on to flatten it. Most of the haystacks are at least 10 feet (3 m) high. They are used to feed livestock.

**Children at play in a farm field**

**Haystacks are used to feed livestock.**

**Forests cover many of Serbia's mountains.**

Lake Palić in Subotica is a popular resort area. Hiking paths, flowering gardens, and sculptures are found throughout the park setting. Water sports, tennis, and hiking are among the activities people enjoy there.

Local legend says that the lake has a monster—like the famed Nessie of Loch Ness. Lake Palić's monster is called the *Palička Neman* (PAH-leech-ka NEH-mahn). The monster is said to be more than 20 feet (6 m) long, with a very long tail. Few people claim to have actually seen it. And those who have seen it didn't get a good look because the Neman appears only when the weather is misty.

### Banat

Banat (BAA-not), also within the province of Vojvodina, has vast plains and marshy valleys. Banat is on the border of Romania. Sand deposits in the southeast form picturesque dunes called *deliblato* (DAY-LEE-blah-toe). Banat is named after the chiefs who once ruled it, the Bans.

## Central Serbia

Šumadija is in the forested central region of Serbia. The word *šuma* (SHOO-ma) means "forest." In the east, the Balkan Mountains form Serbia's border with Bulgaria and Romania, reaching heights of 6,000 feet (1,830 m).

Šumadija is well known for its animal feed (corn, wheat, and hay), mineral water, goose and duck down for jackets, and for its pork and beef. It is also home to Mount Venčac, where beautiful white marble is mined.

Every year in the town of Arandjelovac, a "marble and sound" festival is held. Artists from all over Serbia chisel the glistening white rock and create fabulous forms. For two

## Regional Pride

Every area is known for some special feature. An old Serbian saying describes what the people of central Serbia are known for: *Kroz Bosnu ne pevaj, kroz Šumadiju ne igraj!* or "In Bosnia, don't sing; in Šumadija, don't dance!" It means that the people in Bosnia are good singers and the Šumadija people are good dancers, so don't try to show off your singing and dancing there!

## Djerdap Gorge

Djerdap (JER-dahp) National Park, also known as the Iron Gate Gorge, is a narrow canyon. The Danube River runs through its steep, rocky walls. Djerdap is the longest gorge in Europe. Its rocky walls are up to 1,600 feet (488 m) high, and the Danube reaches a depth there of 330 feet (101 m), making this one of the deepest riverbeds in the world. One of the largest dams in Europe is part of the Djerdap hydroelectric power plant (left), located within the park. The electrical power it produces is used by Yugoslavia and sold to neighboring European countries.

weeks, there are musical concerts and special showings of the sculptures. Then the statues become part of a permanent outdoor exhibit. This town is also famous for Knez Miloš, a mineral-water plant whose waters are sold locally and internationally.

### Water, Water, Everywhere

Large lakes, flowing rivers, cold mountain streams, underground springs, and natural hot springs can be found all over Serbia. The main rivers used for transport are the Danube, Sava, and Morava. Shipping ports in Serbia are located in Belgrade, Novi Sad, Pančevo, and Smederevo. The Danube's primary tributaries are the Sava, Tisa, and Morava Rivers.

Belgrade's location on two rivers makes it an important shipping port.

The Danube River rises in Germany's Black Forest region, then it flows east and empties into the Black Sea off Romania. It is the second-longest river in Europe (about 1,700 miles, or 2,736 km) and the only major European river to flow from west to east. This vital waterway links central Europe with eastern Europe and its longest navigable portion lies within Serbia. Ships and boats carrying goods from around the world travel the 365 miles (588 km) of water that flow through the land.

## Natural Healing

Serbia has more than 140 mineral springs and 53 spas. The spas are health centers and are the oldest tourist resorts in Serbia. These spas use the earth's natural springs to heal a variety of ailments. Vrnjačka Banja, for instance, has three mineral-water springs—one with warm water and two with cold water. The spa treats stomach problems, liver and kidney disorders, and heart conditions.

The hot mineral waters of the spas are said to be especially good for the bones. People come to relax in large tubs of hot water. Some of Serbia's springs have been used since Roman times, when nobles and heads of state visited the spas. They are still popular today. The striking design of some spa and resort buildings demonstrates the talents of Serbia's architects.

Some of Serbia's architects design spectacular modern buildings.

## Kosovo, Where Serbia Began

The southernmost region—Kosovo—is often thought of as the soul of Serbia and the cradle of the Serbian culture. This is where the Serbian empire first began to expand in the twelfth century.

Kosovo, bordering the Albanian Alps to the southwest, is quite rocky. Over the years, many Albanians have crossed the Serbian border to live in Kosovo. The contrast between the northern area of Vojvodina and the southern region of Kosovo is striking. The land is as different as the people. Most people of Albanian descent follow the faith of Islam; most Serbs follow the Christian Orthodox religion. Family structures are also different. Many ethnic Albanians have large families of eight or more children, while most Serbians have smaller families of three or four children.

Kosovo's soil is not good for farming but some crops are grown, mostly maize and rye. Livestock, especially sheep and goats, graze on the fields. Some mineral resources—primarily silver, lead, and zinc—are mined and exported.

**Sheep grazing in the countryside**

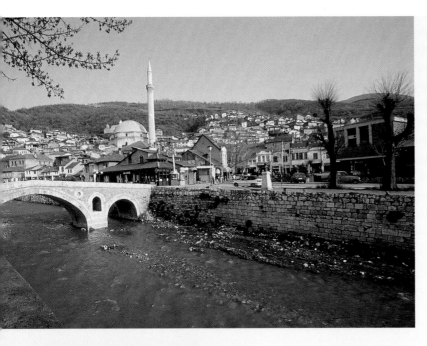

## Looking at Serbia's Cities

Priština (top, left), the capital of Kosovo Province, is near the Kopaonik Mountains. It was a capital of the Serbian empire before the Ottoman Turks' victory at the Battle of Kosovo. A four-teenth-century monastery, Gracanica, is located nearby. The Museum of Kosovo-Metohija and a university are found in Priština. Population (1991 census): 108,083.

Novi Sad is located on the Danube River in Vojvodina Province. The city manufactures porcelain, soap, and textiles. Important sites include the Petrovaradin Fortress, which dates back to Roman times, the Serbian National Theater, and a university. Founded in the seventeenth century, Novi Sad was part of Hungary until the formation of the Kingdom of the Serbs, Croats, and Slovenes in 1918. Population (1991 census): 179,626.

Subotica (bottom, left), the northernmost city in Serbia, is an important commercial, agricultural, and intellectual center. It is also the center of the food industry—agricultural products are processed, packaged, and sold here. Subotica differs from other Serbian cities because it lies on the border of Hungary. It joined Yugoslavia in 1918. The music, architecture, food, and many of the people reflect their Hungarian origins. The street signs, newspapers, and books in this region show that the Hungarian language is as widely used as Serbian. Population (1991 est.): 100,386.

A winter sleigh ride

## Climate: What Do I Wear Today?

The weather in Serbia is much like that of the midwestern United States, although generally less humid. The climate is often called "continental," meaning that winters are very cold and summers are warm. In winter, you need a heavy coat, a hat, mittens, and a scarf, especially in the northern areas. If you

like snow, there's plenty of it in the mountains of central Serbia. In southern Kosovo, the weather is somewhat milder.

Serbia's summers are warm and pleasant, reaching highs of about 80 degrees Fahrenheit (27°C). It gets drier and hotter the farther south you go. On the whole, the mountain regions have cooler, shorter summers and more severe winters.

# Where the Wild Things Grow

Many kinds of trees grow in Serbia, including the mighty oak with its rounded leaves that turn gold and red in the fall. There are also many evergreens, fragrant trees with long green needles that stay on the branches all year round. The sap from pine trees is used to make an incense that smells spicy-sweet. Serbs and other people throughout the world burn incense on special holidays and religious occasions. It is a regular part of Serbian Orthodox Church services.

Trees provide timber for industry as well as food and shelter for animals. Many kinds of wild things climb, crawl, and fly in Serbia's forests. They include deer, foxes, wolves, wild boar, bears, stags, wild lynx, and martens—squirrel-like animals with a long bushy tail and a silky brown coat. Birds, such as grouse, partridges, swallows, nightingales, and woodpeckers, live among the trees.

**A pine marten leaps through the forest.**

*Opposite:* **Sap from pine trees is used to make incense.**

**A wild boar with its young**

**A red fox**

## How Incense Is Made

Incense is often made from tree bark or sap. Pine trees produce resin, a thick brownish sap that oozes out of the tree. In Serbia, people make their own incense by scraping the sap off pine trees. The sticky mass is rolled out like a pencil and pinched into small, pill-sized chunks. It is then sprinkled with corn starch so that the pieces don't stick together and left to air-dry. Sometimes scented oils are poured into the sap before it is rolled out. The incense is burned in small trays called censers.

Where the Wild Things Grow **31**

*Above:* **Partridge prefer open country.**

*Right:* **Jays live in Serbia's forests.**

Serbia has been called the "Garden of the Balkans" because of its many farms. Vegetables and fruits flourish in its nutrient-rich soil. In late spring, sweet red strawberries are the first fruit to appear. Next come cherries and raspberries, followed by peaches, apricots, and blackberries. But no summer in Serbia would be complete without its delicious melons. And when hot summer days give way to fall, it's time for apples and pears.

However, one fruit is honored above all the rest—the plum, the national fruit. Serbia's plum jam and plum brandy (šlivovitz) are enjoyed around the world.

### Fungus Among Us

Mushroom lovers can find plenty of their favorites underneath all those pine trees. From frilly pink mushrooms to honeycombed morel mushrooms, the mountains of Serbia provide the perfect climate for mushrooms to grow. Visitors rely on skilled guides for mushroom-picking expeditions because many mushrooms are poisonous.

In addition to its fruits and vegetables, there's plenty of mooing, cackling, and snorting going on in Serbia. Farm animals are plentiful and the whole family helps care for them. Farmers put bells on their livestock in case they get lost. The tinkling of these bells is as much a part of the countryside as the wild things that grow there.

Oxen help this farmer work his land.

**A shepherd in traditional peasant dress**

Villages are called *selos* (SELL-ohs). Some of the older village women still dress in traditional peasant garb—a long black skirt, a plain blouse, and a head scarf. You might see one of these women walking with a herd of animals—with an ax slung over her shoulder. She uses the ax to chop off tree branches for her animals. Goats and sheep love to munch on leafy twigs.

The national symbol of Serbia is the double-headed white eagle—an ancient artistic creation. It appears on Serbia's coat of arms (left). The symbol comes from the Nemanja Dynasty, a royal family that expanded Serbian territory in the twelfth century. This mythical eagle is thought to be the king of animals.

Dogs, cats, and fish are the most common pets. In farming areas, pets are rarely allowed inside the house. The little Pekinese dog is popular in the city and country alike. But people also keep dalmatians (from the former Yugoslav republic of Dalmatia), rottweilers, German shepherds, huskies, and many mixed breeds. All dogs are required to have yearly shots. They do not wear dog tags, but numbers are tattooed on the inside of a dog's ear instead.

## Belgrade National Zoo

When you think of a zoo, you usually think of exotic animals such as lions, elephants, and ostriches. And the Belgrade Zoo, called the "Goodwill Garden," certainly has all of these. But it also has a section for dogs. There you can see the Sop, the Serbian defense dog—a mixed breed of mastiff, Bosnian wolf, and terrier. The breeds were selected to produce a dog that would be smart, fast, and strong. These brown or black dogs have thick, furry coats and weigh up to 130 pounds (59 kg).

Agriculture has been an important economic activity here for centuries. The main crops are corn, wheat, potatoes, grapes, and animal feed. In addition to modern, large-scale farming, most people have their own small gardens. Even in the city, people grow tomatoes, peppers, and fruit trees.

Unlike in the United States, where grassy lawns often surround a house, gardens in Serbia are filled with flowers. The summer air is sweet with their scent.

Of course, all those trees and flowers attract bees. Because bees cross-pollinate plants, many fruit growers keep them for this purpose. An added bonus is the delicious honey the bees produce. These bees are kept in small wooden boxes where they deposit their nectar into honeycombs. You can see these bee boxes all over Serbia.

## Rock of Ages

Rocks may seem worthless, but they often contain hidden treasures. The Serbian mountains are filled with mineral deposits of coal, iron, lead, copper, and zinc. In Vojvodina, oil and natural gas deposits lie within the rock. These substances and minerals are mined and processed in factories. Rocks can also tell tales—if you know how to read their language.

Fossils found in rocks are like geological history books. Scientists who study these rocks have discovered that millions of years ago, the entire Balkan region was a tropical garden complete with palm trees. Evidence of this has been found in fossil spores from Fruška Gora all the way south to

*Opposite:* **A nun wearing a protective veil displays a honeycomb.**

Montenegro. Some remains are between 180 million and 200 million years old, making them part of what is called the Old Jurassic Period, a time when dinosaurs roamed the earth.

## Battlefield Flower

Serbia has no official national flower, but many people love the *"božur,"* or red peony. Legend has it that the flower turned from white to red because of the blood shed during the Battle of Kosovo in 1389.

## Natural Sculptures

Many of the formations inside caves take on familiar forms. The names of the groupings inside Rajko's Cave in eastern Serbia describe their shapes: the Egyptian Goddess, the Snail, Stump with Mushrooms, and Sleeping Bear. Rajko's Cave has the most interesting cave formations in the region.

## Caves and Karst

Many caves and geological formations known as *karst* are found in Serbia. Karst—a collapsed limestone—has created many underground streams, caves, and craters. The Mermerna (Marble) Cave near Priština is made up of marble cliffs formed by the metamorphosis of limestone, a rare phenomenon. The ceiling is covered with stalactites, which are icicle-shaped masses of calcium carbonate. The pillars in the cave reach heights of up to 6 feet (1.8 m) and are covered with spikes, which is a special oddity of the cave. The colors inside the cave range from white to red with many shades in between.

# When Serbia Began

Historians study the past to help us understand the people, places, and events of earlier times. Archaeologists are like historians who study the remains of ancient cultures. They dig carefully into the earth looking for clues to the past.

## The First People

THE EARLIEST SIGNS OF LIFE IN SERBIA ARE found in an area around the Danube River. The Lepenski Vir culture developed there between 7000 and 6000 B.C. Its discovery in 1965 caused much excitement among scholars, and it turned out to be one of the most important prehistoric sites in Europe.

Lepenski Vir is located in Djerdap National Park. The site is significant because it shows that there were permanent settlements in the area. Elsewhere in Europe at that time, people were nomadic hunters who used only temporary shelters. This area of the Danube is rich in fish and other wildlife, so the easy access to food and water allowed people to settle there.

Archaeologists have found rock sculptures, jewelry, tools, and even carved plaques with raised symbols that look like letters. The symbols are thought to be an early form of written communication, making this culture quite advanced for its time. Lepenski Vir is believed to be the oldest settlement in Europe.

Rock sculptures at Lepenski Vir

*Opposite:* Tsar Lazar is honored on the 600-year anniversary of the Battle of Kosovo.

## Serbs and Slavs

Most Serbians are of Slavic descent, but there is some debate as to the origins of the Slavs. Did they migrate from the Carpathian Mountains, or did they come from the early settlements around the Danube River? No one knows for sure. But we do know that some early Slavs were farmers and herders. Beginning about A.D. 150, these Slavic tribes began to migrate. To the north, they followed the rivers through the forests of Russia. To the west, they met up with Germanic and Celtic tribes and occupied much of Central Europe. By the seventh century, the Slavs had reached as far south as the Adriatic Sea. Today, Slavic people live all over the world.

## Establishment of Serbia

There's no exact date when this area became known as Serbia. As the Serbian empire expanded, the people wanted to gain their independence from outside rulers. Those rulers, the Byzantine Empire, weren't going to let go without a fight, of course. To understand what was happening when Serbia sought independence, we need an understanding of what life was like at that time.

Imagine the Balkan region as the middle of a giant chessboard where players are constantly moving around, trying to gain territory for their side. In the fourteenth century A.D., there was one dominant empire—the Byzantine Empire. The Ottoman Turks were newcomers to the region. They came from Asia Minor, a peninsula that is part of

**Bogomils**

The Bogomils were members of a religious sect that thrived in the Balkans between the tenth and fifteenth centuries. Bogomils were dualists—they believed that God has two sons, Satan and Jesus Christ.

Some Bogomils also may have worshiped the sun, which they called *Bal*, meaning "god of the light." Some scholars say the word *Balkan* comes from the Bogomil word *Bal*.

Turkey today. Both groups wanted to expand their power, and they battled for control of the Balkans.

Before the first century A.D., the Roman Empire ruled much of southern Europe, including the Balkans. It was a large area to control effectively, so the Roman Empire was divided into two parts—east and west. In A.D. 330, Emperor Constantine established Constantinople in Asia Minor

The Turkish conquest of Constantinople in 1453

on the site of the ancient city of Byzantium. This is why the eastern Roman empire is also called the Byzantine Empire.

As the western portion of the Roman Empire grew weaker, the eastern part took control. By the fourth century, the Byzantine Empire controlled parts of Asia Minor.

In the fourteenth century, another group began to gain power in the region. Known as the Ottoman Turks, they came from the Middle East around Baghdad. The Byzantines were Christian and the Ottoman Turks were Muslim, so their religious beliefs were very different. Eventually, the Ottoman Turks took over much of the Byzantine Empire in Asia Minor.

## Golubac Fortress

Built in the fourteenth century on high cliffs overlooking the Danube River, Golubac Fortress guards the entrance to the Iron Gate Gorge. The scene of many battles, Golubac is one of the finest medieval fortresses still standing in Serbia.

Religion was a strong controlling factor in these two empires. There was no separation between church and state back then. In fact, for a state to be recognized, its ruler had to name an independent church. Emperors built large churches and monasteries to establish their power. In Serbia today you can visit many churches that date back to the twelfth century. The Serbian Orthodox Church was founded by Saint Sava in 1219.

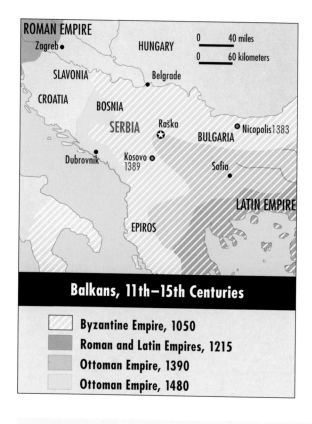

### Balkans, 11th–15th Centuries

- Byzantine Empire, 1050
- Roman and Latin Empires, 1215
- Ottoman Empire, 1390
- Ottoman Empire, 1480

### Rise of the Medieval Serbian State—Twelfth Century

During this period, Serbia wanted to break away from the Byzantine Empire. In the twelfth century, the Hungarians to the north of Serbia waged war against the Byzantine Empire. That battle weakened the Byzantine Empire and diverted its attention from Serbia. Serbia saw an opportunity to build itself up.

### Raška, the Center of Expansion

Serbia was organized into small clans with Raška as the main province. A town called Ras stands today in south-central Serbia. It was in this town that Serbia took root and expanded.

Stefan Nemanja, a clan leader, united all the smaller clans. In 1159 he became grand *župan* (zhupan), or leader of the region. He is considered the first great ruler of Serbia. The Byzantine Empire was still in control, but it had problems in the north with Hungary and was losing its grip. Nemanja cleverly convinced the rulers of the empire

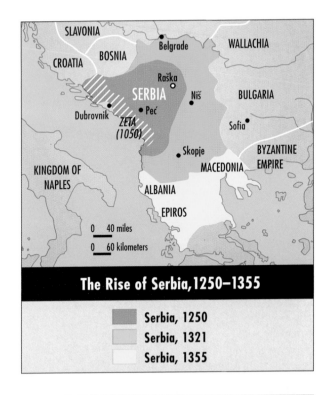

**The Rise of Serbia, 1250–1355**

- Serbia, 1250
- Serbia, 1321
- Serbia, 1355

**Saint Sava and Saint Simeon**

that he would help them keep their hold on the north, so they put him in charge. Nemanja, however, had other plans.

By organizing the local people and uniting the smaller clans, Nemanja made them stronger. Their Christian Orthodox faith helped to keep the people organized and unified. The Serbians challenged the Byzantine Empire. After several battles, they defeated the Byzantine army and formed the country of Serbia.

At the age of eighty-two, Nemanja stepped down from the throne and passed rulership to his middle son, also named Stefan. In 1220, Stefan the Second became king of Serbia. He was known as "Stefan the First Crowned."

The elder Nemanja and his wife devoted the rest of their lives to the Eastern Orthodox Church. They joined their youngest son, Sava, at the "Holy Mountain." Mount Athos, in northern Greece, was the center of the Eastern Orthodox religion. Nemanja later achieved sainthood as Saint Simeon. His son Sava also became a saint.

## The Golden Age of Serbia

Beginning with Stefan the Second, the Nemanja Dynasty ruled Serbia for the next 200 years. During this time, many things changed for the better. Serbian territory expanded and great cities were built. Trade and commerce developed. The rivers that ran through the region became waterways for international transportation.

Serbia became a recognized cultural and political force. Monasteries, especially in Kosovo, flourished as centers of Christian Orthodox teachings. The architecture of and the frescoes within the churches are evidence of the Serbian people's faith and artistry. This "Golden Age" of Serbia continues to be a source of pride to many Serbians today.

### Important Dates in Serbia's History

| | |
|---|---|
| 1159 | Nemanja Dynasty begins. |
| 1219 | Saint Sava establishes the Serbian Orthodox Church. |
| 1220 | Stefan Nemanja is crowned as Serbia's first king. |
| 1389 | Battle of Kosovo |
| 1389–1815 | Ottoman Empire rules Serbia. |
| 1804 | Serbian peasant George Petrović leads uprising against the Turks. |
| 1815 | Serbian leader Miloš Obrenović leads second revolt. |
| 1878 | Serbia regains independence following the Ottoman Empire's defeat by Russia and Serbia. |
| 1912 | During Balkan Wars, Serbia and other Balkan countries gain control of most Ottoman Empire possessions in Europe. |
| 1914 | Austria declares war on Serbia, starting World War I (1914–1918). |
| 1918 | Kingdom of Serbs, Croats, and Slovenes is formed. |
| 1929 | The kingdom is renamed Yugoslavia. |
| 1945 | Serbia becomes one of the republics of the Socialist Federal Republic of Yugoslavia. |
| 1989 | Slobodan Milošević, a Serbian nationalist, becomes president of Serbia. |
| 1990 | Serbia dissolves Kosovo's parliament and ends Communist Party monopoly of power. |
| 1991 | Croatia and Slovenia declare their independence from Yugoslavia. |
| 1992 | Federal Republic of Yugoslavia is formed as self-proclaimed successor to the Socialist Federal Republic of Yugoslavia. |
| 1996 | Milošević nullifies election results when his opposition wins. Protests and demonstrations follow. |
| 1997 | Milošević is elected president of the new Yugoslavia. |

Serbs exported animals, cheese, fur, and honey. From the mountains, they extracted gold, silver, and copper, also for export. They imported textiles, salt, and spices. Germany, Italy, and the Near East all traded with Serbia.

The Nemanja Dynasty built many monasteries. The most spectacular, Studenica, was built in 1183. It still stands today. Throughout the history of medieval Serbia, Studenica was the most famous. It was the home of the elder Stefan Nemanja, and of his son Sava, the first Serbian archbishop. Because of its extraordinary artistic and cultural value, the complex is now under the protection of UNESCO, an agency of the United Nations.

## Studenica

The Studenica Monastery complex is a place where monks study, live, and pray. It is made of gleaming white marble taken from the nearby hills. The windows and doorways are beautifully carved. The frescoes (watercolors painted onto wet plaster) were the first to have Cyrillic lettering, the alphabet developed for the Slavic language.

## Serbian Reign Expands

The Serbian Empire eventually controlled most of what is now Yugoslavia (Serbia and Montenegro) and Albania and reached as far south as Greece. Stefan Dušan was the last great ruler of the Nemanja Dynasty. During his reign (1331–1355), Serbia had a mixed Serbian and Greek population. Dušan was called Tsar of the Serbs and Greeks, but his empire fell apart after his death.

While Serbia was gaining territory, however, the Ottoman Empire was also expanding. By the fourteenth century, the Ottoman Turks would slap Serbia down and forever change the course of Serbian history.

## The Fall of Serbia

On June 28, 1389, the Ottoman army was at Serbia's gates in Kosovo. They demanded that the Serbs surrender. The Serbian forces were much smaller and would most certainly be crushed by the Turks. But this was more than a battle between a small army and a larger one—it was a war between Christianity and Islam. Serb military leader Tsar Lazar saw his choice as this: He could either surrender to the earthly kingdom, or sacrifice for the heavenly kingdom in the name of Christianity.

The battle was fought on the field of Kosovo, which means "field of blackbirds." Tsar Lazar led his army into certain defeat. The battle was devastating to the Serbians, who lost most of their elite ruling class. The area then became a Turkish *pashalik*, or province. The Ottomans spread farther

## Tsarina Milica

After Tsar Lazar was killed in battle, his wife, Tsarina (Empress) Milica, took over. She ruled the land until her son was old enough to assume that responsibility. Ruling was generally a man's job back then, but the tsarina was a diplomat. She also cared for war widows, founded monasteries, and encouraged nuns to create intricate embroidered tapestries. Some of those fine old tapestries can be seen in museums today.

and farther into Serbian territory, taking over the land and enslaving the people. By 1459, the Ottoman Empire's invasion of Serbia was complete. The nearly 500 years of Turkish rule that followed the Battle of Kosovo severely diminished Serbia's own economic, cultural, and civic development.

Through that tragedy, Serbians developed an even stronger national and cultural unity. To them, Kosovo had the same religious significance that Jerusalem had for the Israelites. It instilled a stubborn pride and a strong spirit in the people. That spirit eventually would rise up and once again demand freedom.

*The Kosovo Maiden,* by Uroš Predic

### The Battle of Kosovo

The commemoration of the 1389 Battle of Kosovo is still a solemn holiday in Serbia. Many forms of art were inspired by that battle. Poetry, ballads, and paintings have preserved the story from one generation to the next.

### The Fall of the Serbian Empire

*Lord, my God which shall by my portion,*
*Which my choice of these two proffer'd kingdoms?*
*Shall I choose God's kingdom, shall I rather*
*Choose an earthly one? For what is earthly*
*Is all fleeting, vain, and unsubstantial.*
*Heavenly things are lasting, firm, eternal.*

## Freedom Regained

The Serbs finally regained their freedom in the nineteenth century, but only after more bloodshed. It took many battles to free themselves from the Turks. The pivotal battle, led by Miloš Obrenović in 1815, freed Serbia of Turkish domination. Obrenović became prince in 1817, and Serbia was granted limited self-government. But it had lost most of the territory it once held.

During the Russo-Turkish War of 1877–1878, Serbia and Russia joined together to defeat Turkey in the Balkans. The 1878 Congress of Berlin gave Serbia back its independence— but not all of its land. Austria took control of Bosnia and Herzegovina, where many Serbs lived. Serbia's relations with Austria became very tense.

The Congress of Berlin had a number of results. The Turks lost most of their European territory, Russian influence was decreased in the Middle East, and the power of Austria-Hungary

Miloš Obrenović led the battle that freed Serbia of Turkish domination.

**The Congress of Berlin, 1878**

and Great Britain was increased. Neither the Balkan countries nor Russia was satisfied with what it got. This dissatisfaction created tension among countries and was among the main causes of World War I (1914–1918).

In 1912, Serbs took an active part in the Balkan Wars, which gave them international recognition as well as territory in Macedonia. Serbs also regained other lands, including Kosovo, the cradle of their civilization. Austria was alarmed by this rise in Serbian power.

## World War I

*Trust* was not a word that applied to the Serbian and Austrian relationship. In 1914 in Sarajevo, Bosnia, a Serb nationalist named Gavrilo Princip assassinated Austrian Archduke Francis Ferdinand. The Austrian government held Serbia responsible. They declared war and invaded Serbia. The Serbs fought hard, but by December the country was occupied by foreigners once again.

The assassination of Francis Ferdinand, from a painting by I. B. Hazelton

For the Serbs, freedom and independence were hard won and difficult to hold on to. They had just ended 500 years of foreign rule and now, once again, they were under the thumb of another nation. They were not alone; other Slavs were also governed by the mighty Austro-Hungarian Empire. Together with other Slavic people, the Serbs eventually would find a way out.

## The Creation of Yugoslavia

In 1918, World War I ended. The leaders of several groups of people decided that it was better for Slavs to be united than to fall prey to outside powers. Serbia, Croatia, Slovenia, Bosnia and Herzegovina, Macedonia, and Montenegro joined together as the Kingdom of the Serbs, Croats, and Slovenes, which became Yugoslavia in 1929.

Yugoslavia, 1929

## Assassination of a King

In October 1934, King Aleksandar of Yugoslavia went to Marseilles, France, to broaden the friendship between Serbia and France. He was assassinated there by an agent of the Croat Ustasha extremist group. The Ustasha were Fascists who opposed Aleksandar's policies and sought independence for Croatia. By murdering the 46-year-old king, they hoped to disorganize Yugoslavia and achieve their goal. Citizens of both Serbia and Croatia were outraged by the act, however, and Yugoslavia remained intact until World War II (1939–1945). This photo was taken only minutes before Aleksandar's death.

Yugoslavia was a union of many peoples. Most of the people were Slavic in origin, but they had spent centuries under different governments and different lifestyles. Disagreements arose about culture, religion, and how to run a country. The Slovenes and Croatians were Roman Catholic, while the Serbs were Orthodox. In addition, after 500 years of Turkish rule, many Slavs had been converted to the Islamic religion, so now there was a sizable Muslim community as well. The idea of unity among these three groups of people looked simple enough on paper, but it would prove to be more difficult in real life.

The leaders of the newly formed Yugoslavia couldn't agree on the form of government. Disagreement was especially strong between the Serbs and the Croats. However, Serbia had a strong history as an independent state, and a large percentage of the Yugoslavian population was Serbian. The government became a constitutional monarchy with a Serb by the name of Aleksandar Karadjordjević as king. Belgrade became the capital of the new country.

The main problem in Europe and the Balkans during World War II was the rise of Fascist Italy and Nazi Germany. In March 1941, Serbia closed its borders to stop Germany from invading and reaching farther down into the Balkans. But this did not stop the Nazis. Hitler bombed Belgrade a month later.

The Germans also marched into Croatia, where they were considered liberators—troops that would free Croatia from the hands of Serbia as the head of Yugoslavia. The Yugoslav government fell apart, and people began to fight over whom would be in charge next. The stakes were high because the winner of the battle would rule the land. So Serbia was in a state of civil war as well as in a world war.

## Outside Support of Internal Conflict

A group of Serb fighters called Četniks resisted the German invasion. They were led by Colonel Draža Mihajlović *(seated, second from left)*, and at first their efforts were supported by the British. The Četniks battled not only the Germans but also another group of Yugoslav fighters called the Partisans, who had their own ideas of how the government should be run. The Partisans were essentially Communists, led by Josip Broz Tito. Eventually, the British thought the Partisans were doing a better job at fighting the Germans, so in 1943, the British switched their support from the Četniks to the Partisans. With that kind of power behind them, the Partisans won. The new Yugoslavia would be governed by Tito.

Before the war ended, a reign of terror as shocking as Hitler's murderous treatment of the Jews took place in Serbia. Croatia, supported by Italy, was turned into a pro-Fascist puppet state. The recruited military, called the Ustasha, were led by nationalists in Croatia. They were terrorists, like the Nazis, and they sought to get rid of all Serbs, Jews, and Gypsies. Many people were brutally murdered or forced to convert to Catholicism. By the end of the war, some 750,000 people were murdered in this Serbian holocaust.

## The Second Yugoslavia, 1945–1991

The new Yugoslavia, now in the hands of Tito, suppressed the nationalist spirit of all people "in the name of brotherhood and unity." People were not allowed to talk about the terrible war that had just ended. Imagine getting into a fight with your neighbors and being told to just forget about it, instead of trying to make peace with them. There was no resolution—no attempt was made to repair the hurt feelings and learn to live together again.

The government became a one-party Communist rule and Tito was declared president for life. His picture was displayed in all public environments: stores, schools, factories, and offices. Yugoslavia became the Socialist Federal Republic of Yugoslavia.

Under Communism, the government owns everything: industries, businesses, schools, hospitals, and the media. There is no such thing as a privately owned business. The Serbian word for government, *država*, is related to the word meaning "hold." In this case, the government certainly did hold everything.

**Josip Broz Tito
(1892–1980)**

Josip Broz was born on May 7, 1892, in Kumrovec, Croatia (then part of Austria-Hungary). His mother was Slovene and his father was a Croatian blacksmith. In the early 1920s, he worked as an illegal Communist party organizer. After he served a prison term (1929–1934), he took the name "Tito" as an alias and went to Moscow to work for the Communist International. Tito ruled Yugoslavia for 35 years. He died in 1980.

A celebration of Tito's 85th birthday in Belgrade

In 1946, the Yugoslav government adopted a constitution that was similar to that of the Soviet Union, but with an important difference. Unlike other Eastern European Communists, the Yugoslavs did not allow the Soviets to control them. In 1948, Josef Stalin, the Communist dictator of the Soviet Union, could no longer tolerate Tito's resistance. He expelled the Yugoslav Party from the Cominform, the Communist Information Bureau.

## The Cominform

The Cominform (Communist Information Bureau) was an organization that included the governing Communist parties of Eastern Europe plus the Communist parties of France and Italy. It was an instrument of control, and its main activity was publishing Soviet propaganda. Formed in 1947, it included Bulgaria, Czechoslovakia, France, Hungary, Italy, Poland, Romania, the Soviet Union, and Yugoslavia.

## The Nonaligned Movement

During the Cold War following World War II, there were two power blocs in the world. One was led by the United States and the other by the Soviet Union. The Nonaligned Movement was made up of countries that did not wish to be tied to either of those major powers.

**The Balkans Today**

Yugoslavia began to form its own version of socialism. Tito created workers' councils, a system of self-management in which the participants could decide on many procedures for the enterprises or offices they worked for. Tito avoided association with both the Soviets and the West. He helped to establish the Nonaligned Movement, which put him on the world stage.

After Tito died in 1980, Yugoslavia was up for grabs once again. Who would govern the country? The government adopted a "collective presidency," meaning that each Yugoslav republic would have its own representative and together they would decide what was best for Yugoslavia as a whole. The president of Yugoslavia was selected from this collective group. The position of president would rotate among the republics. That way, each republic eventually would have its leader as president. That seemed to work well for a time. But by 1990, conflicts arose again.

### Yugoslavia Splits Again

Serbia wanted to hold the Yugoslav republics together, but several republics wanted out. Slovenia was the first to go, followed by Croatia. The difficulty was that people of different ethnic groups lived all over Yugoslavia. This was especially true in Bosnia and Herzegovina, which had no clear ethnic majority. Serbs, Muslims, and Croats fought a bitter battle for control of this region.

The civil war of the 1990s was tragic for Bosnia and Herzegovina. It was a brutal war, like all wars, and many innocent people lost their lives. It's important to remember that wars are made by politicians. Most Croatians, Serbians, and Muslims did not want this war, but they had little choice.

### A Sliver of Yugoslavia Remains

By the end of April 1992, Serbia and Montenegro declared themselves the Federal Republic of Yugoslavia (FRY), but the United Nations (UN) refused to recognize the country. However, some countries, including Russia, China, and Japan, do acknowledge this new FRY.

Slobodan Milošević became president of Serbia in 1989 and, in 1997, he became president of the FRY. A former Communist bureaucrat, Milošević used his control of the media, government appointments, the police, and the military to build a Serbian radical nationalist movement.

Men wounded in Yugoslavia's civil war await their evacuation.

# From Unity to Breakup

Serbia and Montenegro are the two remaining republics that form the Federal Republic of Yugoslavia (FRY). They have renewed the system of government, and daily life continues.

*Opposite:* **The Federal Assembly building in Belgrade**

ONE UNFORTUNATE RESULT OF WAR IS THAT MANY PEOPLE have to leave their homes. Some 600,000 refugees of all ethnic origins now live in Serbia. The government has given them some support in terms of food and shelter, but most refugees are helped by their families and neighbors.

**The legislature in session**

### Government of the Federal Republic of Yugoslavia

Serbia is an important part of the FRY. The president of the FRY is elected by the Federal Assembly for a term of four years. Slobodan Milošević, a Serb, was elected president in 1997.

The Federal Assembly is located in the center of Belgrade. Belgrade is the capital city, the political and administrative center of the FRY, and the seat of the federal, republic, and city administration. The Federal Assembly consists of two houses—the Chamber of Citizens and the

## Belgrade: Did You Know This?

In Serbian, Belgrade is *Beograd*, meaning "white city." The city has been known as Belgrade since the ninth century. Its former name is Singidunum. It was first settled in the third or fourth century B.C. by a Celtic tribe, the Scordisci. A large stone fortress surrounds the old part of the city. One of the largest fortifications of its kind in the world, it stands on a bluff above the meeting point of the Danube and Sava Rivers. Those rivers flow through countries that lie north and south of Serbia, making Belgrade a key transportation center and a very valuable place. As a result, the city has been captured sixty times and destroyed thirty-eight times.

A sixteenth-century mosque, a nineteenth-century cathedral, and the Serbian Academy of Sciences are located in Belgrade. Karadjordjević Royal Palace on Dedinje Hill overlooks the city. Once a museum, it became the residence of President Milošević in 1997. Today 1,602,226 people live in this modern city complete with many fine museums and shops.

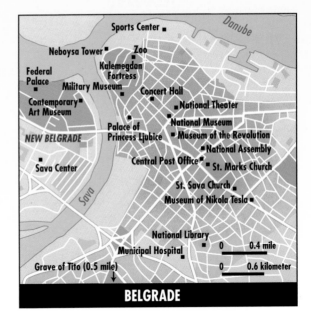

Chamber of Republics. Its members are elected as federal deputies for a term of four years. The Chamber of Citizens has 138 deputies, each representing 65,000 voters.

Under the present constitution, 30 deputies come from Montenegro and 108 from Serbia. The deputies of the Chamber of Republics are elected by the republic assemblies—20 from each republic. Eleven political parties—seven from Serbia and four from Montenegro—take part in the Federal Assembly.

The Federal Court decides cases that require the application of federal law, such as property disputes among the republics, as well as cases within the republics and the federal state. This is similar to the duties of the U.S. Supreme Court. The judges of the Federal Court are elected by the Federal Assembly for a term of nine years.

## Government of the Republic of Serbia

Serbia's government structure is similar to the FRY's. It has three branches—executive, legislative, and judicial. The executive branch is made up of the president and the prime minister, deputy prime ministers, and ministers. The president is elected by the people for a five-year term and may serve no more than two terms. All ministers are elected by the members of the National Assembly.

The National Assembly is the legislative branch of Serbia's government. It has only one house, whose 250 members are elected by the people for four-year terms. The judicial branch is independent of the executive and legislative branches. It includes the Supreme Court of Serbia, the Constitutional Court of Serbia, and the lower courts.

## National Flag

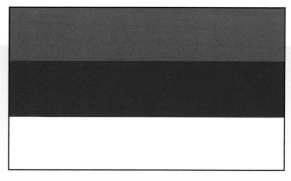

The national flag of Serbia has three horizontal bands of red, blue, and white. An old folk song describes the colors this way:

*Crvena je krvca bila po Kosovu što se lila;*
*Plavo nebo ko sloboda ideal je srpskog roda;*
*Belim mlekom majka mila i mene je zadojila;*
*Jedan venac—tri su boje, trobojnica srpska to je.*

*"Red for the blood that was shed in Kosovo,*
*Blue for heavenly freedom which is Serbia's right,*
*White is for mother's pure milk that gives life;*
*One flag with three colors united, that is Serbia."*

## NATIONAL GOVERNMENT OF SERBIA

### Executive Branch

| PRESIDENT | PRIME MINISTER |
| --- | --- |
| | DEPUTY PRIME MINISTERS (5) |
| | MINISTERS (30) |

### Legislative Branch

NATIONAL ASSEMBLY (250)

### Judicial Branch

CONSTITUTIONAL COURT OF SERBIA

SUPREME COURT OF SERBIA

## The Kosovo Policy

Kosovo was part of the medieval kingdom of Serbia. It is in the southernmost part of Serbia, bordering Albania. The majority of people who live in Kosovo today are ethnic Albanians. Many Kosovo Albanians have been unhappy under Serbian rule. Tensions increased in 1990 when the Serbian government revoked Kosovo's autonomous status.

In the late 1990s, extremist Kosovo Albanians formed an illegal army to try to separate forcibly from Serbia. The inter-

### Slobodan Milošević

Slobodan Milošević was born in 1941. He graduated with a degree in law from Belgrade University in 1964. There he met Ivan Stambolić, who became his friend and mentor. In 1986 Stambolić became president of Serbia, and Milošević replaced him as head of the Serbian Communist Party. At that time, tensions grew between the Serbs in Kosovo and the ethnic Albanians who lived there. Milošević built on these tensions, and Stambolić's regime was criticized for its failure to defend Serbian interests in Kosovo. A few months later, Stambolić was removed from office. In 1989, Milošević was elected president of Serbia.

The civil war in the early 1990s, along with the lack of economic reform and the Milošević family's growing stockpile of money and power, distanced the president from the people. In 1996, citizens voiced their outrage with Milošević's policies by electing politicians who opposed him. Milošević then declared those local elections invalid. For months, thousands of protesters marched in the streets of Belgrade and other cities.

national community did not support this call for separation. Despite attempts to negotiate the situation peacefully, there has been violence in the region. Thousands of Serbs and ethnic Albanians had to leave their homes to escape the fighting. Serbian president Milošević is seeking a compromise solution to the conflict in Kosovo.

The international community is trying to help these groups find a peaceful solution. Some observers fear that the violence might spread into neighboring Albania and Macedonia. If it did reach these ethnically and religiously troubled regions, the conflict could involve nearby countries.

**The town of Prizren, in Kosovo**

In mid-1998, NATO forces representing the international community flew over Albania in an attempt to calm the situation.

*Serbian Interior Ministry Special Police in riot formation in Kosovo try to discourage violence.*

### Armed Forces

Serbia and Montenegro form the Yugoslav army. They have ground forces for internal and border controls, a navy, an air force, and civil defense forces. All males are required to serve twelve months in the army. In addition to a drafted army, there are paid special forces in the army, navy, and air force.

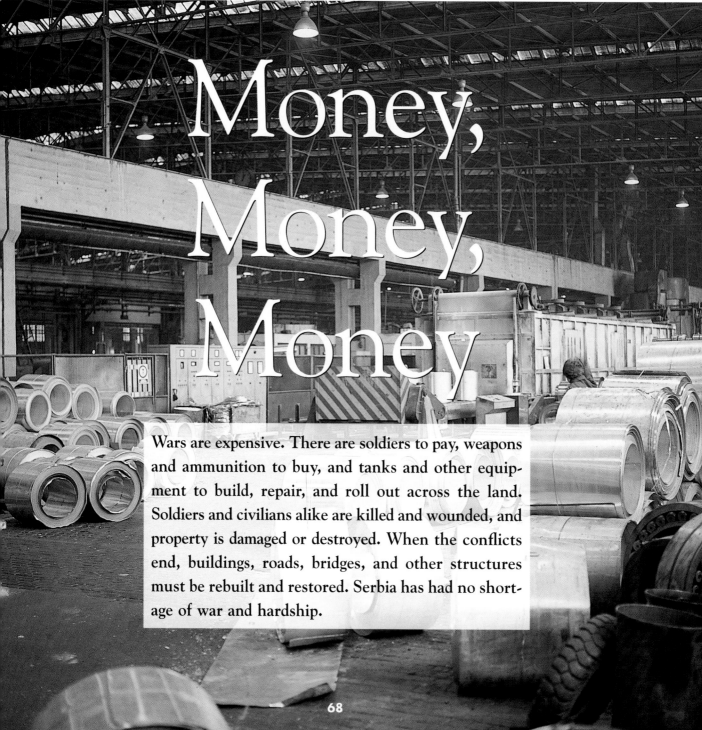

# Money, Money, Money

Wars are expensive. There are soldiers to pay, weapons and ammunition to buy, and tanks and other equipment to build, repair, and roll out across the land. Soldiers and civilians alike are killed and wounded, and property is damaged or destroyed. When the conflicts end, buildings, roads, bridges, and other structures must be rebuilt and restored. Serbia has had no shortage of war and hardship.

*Opposite:* **A metal factory**

THE CIVIL WAR IN THE EARLY 1990S SEVERELY HURT SERBIA'S economy. It has been as damaging to Serbia as the Great Depression of the 1930s was to the economy of the United States. What was it like to live in Serbia in the early 1990s?

**Hungry people line up to receive free bread in Belgrade during the economic crisis.**

It meant long lines at the grocery store, shortages of all kinds, no gasoline at the pumps, and people losing their jobs and their life's savings. The government was slow—or unable—to pay social security checks, and older people who relied on that money had no reliable source of income. But that wasn't the end of it.

### Yugoslavia's Currency

The Yugoslav New Dinar (YD) is Yugoslavia's currency. There are 100 paras in a dinar. The following leaders are shown on Yugoslavian paper money:

**100 dinars**– Dositey Obradović (educator instrumental in establishing high schools and promoting literature and poetry)

**50 dinars**– Miloš Obrenović (prince from 1815 to 1839)

**20 dinars**– Djura Jakšić (famous playwright, poet, and painter)

**10 dinars**– Prince-Bishop Petar Petrović Njegoš (gifted writer/ philosopher/statesman of the nineteenth century; opened the first formal school in 1834)

**5 dinars**– Nikola Tesla (scientist who invented alternating electrical current [AC])

The exchange rate in 1998 was YD10.83 to $U.S.1.

During the civil war, inflation rates soared. Every day, money was worth less and everything cost more. For example, the price of bread could double in a week. Because everything was rationed, people were allowed to buy only one loaf at a time. Essentials like soap and toilet paper became ridiculously expensive. Luxuries like music and trips to the theater were out of reach for many people. A pair of sneakers cost the equivalent of a month's wages.

Life in Serbia would have been even harder without the fertile land. People in rural areas grow a lot of their own food. In season, the earth provides a rich harvest of delicious fruits and vegetables. Fresh water runs from the mountains all year round.

The countryside is filled with grazing sheep, goats, cattle, and lots of pigs, too. Nearly every house has a few chickens pecking around in the yard. In fact, Serbia's economy is based on agriculture and its variety of natural resources.

## Economic Sanctions

During wartime, country people didn't suffer nearly as much as city people. But the farmers could not get their goods to market. They had no gasoline because the United Nations had imposed economic sanctions that made it illegal for other countries to sell gasoline to Serbia. Farmers could still travel by horse and wagon, but that took longer and they couldn't go as far or carry as much as they could with a truck.

### Economics Exercise

What would massive inflation be like for you? Say you could buy a compact disc for $15 one week. The next week, your $15 would be worth only $7, but the CD would cost $30. And prices for everything—food, clothing, medicine, and other essentials, not just luxury goods—would be affected in the same way.

**Horse carts and cars share a road.**

Economic sanctions are a kind of punishment against a country. Serbia was punished by the UN for supporting the Bosnian Serbs during the civil war in the 1990s. The UN imposed a blockade, meaning that Serbia could not trade with other countries. Serbia could not sell its goods, nor could it buy goods from other UN nations.

The goal of economic sanctions is to get the ruler or government of a country to behave in a particular manner, but the sanctions create great hardships for ordinary people. The biggest problem in Serbia is that economic sanctions may

### The Black Market

Black-market trade is the buying and selling of goods without the authority of the government and without paying taxes. For example, people living along the narrowest part of the Danube River in Serbia could easily cross over to Romania, where gasoline was less expensive. Riding in small motorboats, they met in the middle of the river and exchanged empty plastic liter bottles for bottles filled with gasoline. They then sold the gasoline in Serbia for twice what they paid for it. It was a dangerous activity because the highly flammable gasoline was not always stored safely. It was also illegal. Products of all types, from compact discs (left) to medical supplies, are sold on the black market.

A violin maker in Vojvodina

wipe out the middle class. If they go on for too long, you end up with a country that has a small percentage of very rich people. There is so little to go around that people who control the flow of goods may hoard them, then sell them at a very high price. Most citizens may fall into poverty.

## A Changing Economy

People can now own their own businesses. Under the old Yugoslav socialist structure, the government owned everything except small farms, so most people worked for the government. That's no longer the case. People have started companies and opened cafés and stores. It's very exciting. They are working harder than ever and discovering the meaning of a free market economy. Unfortunately, the economic sanctions throughout the 1990s prevented businesses from growing to their full potential.

## Foreign Trade Prior to the Sanctions

Serbia trades with countries both near and far. In 1990, export items included machinery and transportation equipment; manufactured goods like shoes, televisions, cars, and chemicals; and food, beverages, livestock, and minerals. A huge hydroelectric dam built in the Djerdap (Iron Gate Gorge) National Park is one of the largest electrical plants in Europe. It supplies electricity to Yugoslavia and exports it to neighboring countries.

## What Serbia Grows, Makes, and Mines

**Agriculture**
- Wheat
- Maize and corn
- Oil seeds
- Sugar beets
- Fruit

**Manufacturing**
- Food, textile, and metal processing
- Automobiles and agricultural machinery
- Household appliances
- Petroleum products
- Pharmaceuticals

**Mining (1998)**
- Lead
- Copper
- Zinc

## Agriculture

Serbia has a well-distributed rainfall and a long growing season. Most large-scale food production takes place in the northern region of Vojvodina. Cereal production, such as corn and barley, supplies feed for livestock. Large industries also process cotton, oil seeds, and chicory. Serbia also has flour mills, sugar refineries, distilleries, and textile plants.

Vines and fruit trees have been cultivated for more than 2,500 years. Good wines, brandies, and juices come from Fruška Gora and other regions. In addition, many people make juices from their own fruits.

A cow stands in a cornfield east of Belgrade.

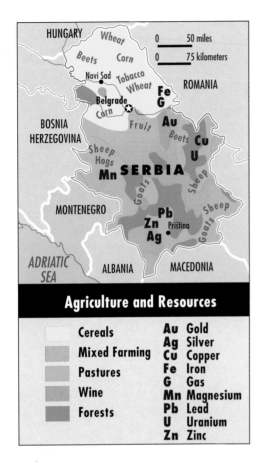

**Agriculture and Resources**

| | | |
|---|---|---|
| Cereals | Au | Gold |
| | Ag | Silver |
| Mixed Farming | Cu | Copper |
| Pastures | Fe | Iron |
| | G | Gas |
| Wine | Mn | Magnesium |
| | Pb | Lead |
| Forests | U | Uranium |
| | Zn | Zinc |

### Miners First

In Novo Brdo, a town where Serbia's biggest silver mine was located, a miniature sculpture from the sixteenth century revealed the Code of Novo Brdo. The code made sure the miners had safe working conditions and required that air shafts be placed in the mines. Mine workers were privileged people at that time. For example, merchants were forbidden to sell food to anyone else if a miner was waiting to buy it.

Kosovo, the southernmost region of Serbia, is the least economically developed. The land is not fertile, but some fruits, vegetables, tobacco, and a small amount of cereals grow there. The mountainous pastures of Kosovo provide good grazing land for sheep and goats. Some of the region's vineyards are famous for their wines.

### Mining

Serbia has many mineral resources in its mountains. The mining industry extracts coal, copper, lead, zinc, nickel, chromium, silver, and even gold. Factories produce steel and aluminum. Serbia is also a major producer of lead, and it has the largest copper mine in Europe.

### Places to Go, Things to Do

Tourism is still only a small part of the economy, but it has great potential for growth. The natural beauty of Serbia offers many outdoor activities, such as hiking, sailing, rafting, and

## Kopaonik Resort

Kopaonik is a popular ski center. Even with some 200 sunny days a year, a blanket of snow lies on this mountain from November till May. Skiers from all over Europe enjoy schussing down its slopes. Come summer, hikers and horseback riders follow the trails. Mountain streams sparkle amid the tall pines, and edible wild fruits and berries are there for the gathering. You may get lost in these hills, but you won't go hungry!

## A Shining Masterpiece in Topola

The Church of St. George and the mausoleum of the Karadjordjević Dynasty was built in the early 1900s on top of Oplenac Hill in the town of Topola. It is a spectacular work of art. The exterior is made of gleaming white marble from the nearby hills. The interior is covered with mosaics, gold, and carved marble. The mosaics are modeled after those in medieval Serbian monasteries, and the pictures are both historic and religious. The mosaics are made of 40 million glass pieces in 15,000 hues.

downhill skiing. Some people visit the northern area to fish and others come to hunt pheasants, partridges, wild duck, hares, and wild boar.

Serbia's natural hot-spring spas are popular health retreats and tourist centers. Entire towns that cater to tourists have sprung up around these natural springs. Visitors also enjoy the many ancient churches and monasteries.

*Opposite:* **Boating near the Sava River**

# Who Lives in Serbia?

Most of the people who live in Serbia are Serbian, but other ethnic groups live there too. The largest groups include Croatians, Hungarians, Romanians, Slovenians, and Albanians. Each group has contributed its own cultural flavor to the cities, towns, and small villages of Serbia.

*Opposite:* **People in traditional dress parade through Belgrade.**

M ANY HUNGARIAN PEOPLE LIVE IN THE NORTHERN province of Vojvodina. Its capital city, Subotica, is very close to the border of Hungary, and you can see the Hungarian influence everywhere. There is a Hungarian theater, and restaurants serve Hungarian dishes such as goulash, a spicy stew. Many people speak Hungarian, and the language is used in newspapers and on street signs.

## The North

## Reading, Writing, Arithmetic

The language known as Serbian is spoken throughout Serbia. It is written in two alphabets—Roman and Cyrillic. Why two? When Croatia was a part of Yugoslavia, the language was known as Serbo-Croatian because the two languages are nearly identical. Croatians were influenced by the Western Roman church, so they used the Roman alphabet. Serbians were influenced by the Eastern part of the Roman Empire, so they used the Cyrillic alphabet associated with that part of the world.

**Population distribution in Serbia**

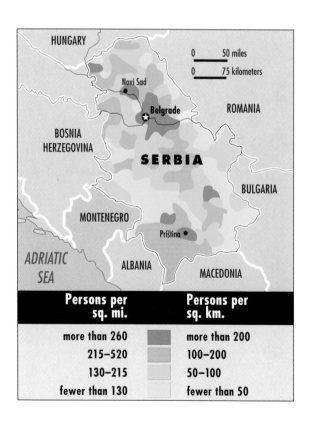

| Persons per sq. mi. | | Persons per sq. km. |
|---|---|---|
| more than 260 | | more than 200 |
| 215–520 | | 100–200 |
| 130–215 | | 50–100 |
| fewer than 130 | | fewer than 50 |

Who Lives in Serbia? **81**

## Who Lives in Serbia?

| | |
|---|---|
| Serbs | 66% |
| Albanians | 17% |
| Hungarians | 4% |
| Muslims | 3% |
| Other | 10% |

The Cyrillic alphabet has 30 letters. Children learn both alphabets in school. Since the split with Croatia in the early 1990s, Serbians tend to use the Cyrillic alphabet more often. Many newspapers, magazines, and street signs appear in Cyrillic. It is the official alphabet.

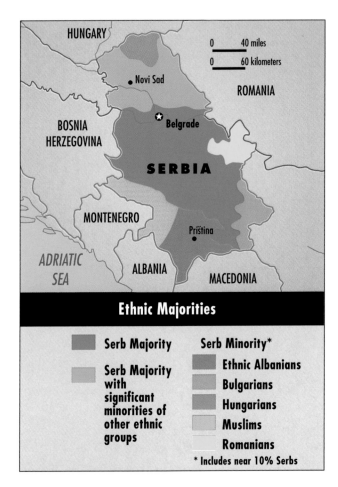

### Ethnic Majorities

Serb Majority

Serb Majority with significant minorities of other ethnic groups

Serb Minority*
Ethnic Albanians
Bulgarians
Hungarians
Muslims
Romanians
* Includes near 10% Serbs

People of all ethnic groups live throughout Serbia, but there are areas where certain groups are concentrated.

## An Alphabet Comparison

| The Roman Alphabet | | The Cyrillic Alphabet | | Pronounced As In |
|---|---|---|---|---|
| A | a | А | а | father |
| B | b | Б | б | beg |
| C | c | Ц | ц | lots |
| Č | č | Ч | ч | chime |
| Ć | ć | Ћ | ћ | tune |
| D | d | Д | д | dog |
| Dž | dž | Џ | џ | joy |
| Đ | đ | Ђ | ђ | dew |
| E | e | Е | е | men |
| F | f | Ф | ф | fish |
| G | g | Г | г | good |
| H | h | Х | х | his |
| I | i | И | и | she |
| J | j | Ј | ј | you |
| K | k | К | к | kind |
| L | l | Л | л | lake |
| Lj | lj | Љ | љ | million |
| M | m | М | м | moon |
| N | n | Н | н | not |
| Nj | nj | Њ | њ | onion |
| O | o | О | о | door |
| P | p | П | п | pen |
| R | r | Р | р | run |
| S | s | С | с | son |
| Š | š | Ш | ш | she |
| T | t | Т | т | tag |
| U | u | У | у | rule |
| V | v | В | в | very |
| Z | z | З | з | zoo |
| Ž | ž | Ж | ж | leisure |

This road sign in neighboring Macedonia is written in two alphabets.

СВЕТИ КИРИЛ
И МЕТОДИЈ

The Cyrillic alphabet has a long history closely tied to Orthodox Christianity. That religion was introduced to the Slavs by Greek Byzantine missionaries in the ninth and tenth centuries. At first, the missionaries conducted their church services in Greek, which very few Slavs could understand. At that time, the people of Serbia spoke many Slavic dialects. They could understand one another, but some words and phrases were different from one village to the next. They had no common language or alphabet to unite them. Two brothers decided to change that.

The Greek missionaries Cyril and Methodius got to work and created what is now known as the Cyrillic alphabet. Thus began the literary language of the church, called Old Church Slavonic. The same idea—of one language uniting many peoples—worked in Western Europe. In Rome, Latin served that purpose.

## One Sound for One Letter

"Write it the way you speak. Read it as it is written." That was Vuk Karadzić's philosophy for spelling. In the nineteenth century, Karadzic' reformed the Serbian language and wrote the first dictionary using a phonetic spelling system. This greatly simplified the language, making it easier to learn. Each word is spelled just as it sounds. Every letter has just one sound. The emphasis is generally on the first syllable.

In English, vowels can be long or short, and there are silent letters, like "gh" in the word "thigh." If English were a phonetic language, "thigh" would simply be spelled "thi."

A few English phrases are respelled from a Serbian point of view below. Sound them out to see what they mean. (Hint: a "j" is pronounced like a "y" and "i" is pronounced "ee.")

Tu bojs end tri gerls

Bi gud to jur self

Aj dont no

---

### English Is Everywhere

Other languages are spoken in Serbia, including English. Though most people are not fluent in English, English words are often used. Words like *hamburger*, *computer*, and *drugstore* are used in everyday conversation. American culture has also influenced lifestyles in Serbia, especially in the cities. You'll see American-style dress and fast-food restaurants, and hear plenty of American music. Of course, the influences of other European nations are also very strong, and you can buy Italian shoes, German electronics, and lots of delicious Swiss chocolates.

**A young girl on a farm in southern Serbia**

*Opposite:* **A statue of Cyril and Methodius, creators of the Cyrillic alphabet**

## Metric Conversion

How many kilograms do you weigh? If you weigh 100 pounds, you would weigh 45 kilograms.
1 pound = 0.45 kilogram
100 x 0.45 = 45

## Population of Serbia's Largest Cities (1991 census)

| | |
|---|---|
| Belgrade | 1,602,226 |
| Novi Sad | 179,626 |
| Niš | 175,391 |
| Kragujevac | 147,305 |

Shoes are left in the doorway of this home.

### Arithmetic

Like most of the world, Serbia uses the metric system. Weight is measured in kilograms, distances in kilometers, and temperatures in Celsius. The metric system was introduced in France in 1799. Most countries adopted it as the common system of weights and measures. All countries use the metric system as an international standard for science. The United States has tried many times to convert to the metric system but it hasn't succeeded yet.

### Hospitality Serbian Style

Despite outside influences, Serbia has kept its own customs. For example, when you enter a Serbian home for the first time, it is customary to bring a small gift, such as flowers, a bottle of wine, or some chocolates for the children. You would probably take off your shoes when you enter and leave them

at the doorway. Slippers would be provided for you to wear. Most people don't go barefoot in their homes.

In Serbia, it is customary to serve something whenever guests come to visit. You might be served a sweet called *slatko,* which is a delicious fruit preserve, often made of strawberries. In both the city and the country, slatko is often served on a small silver tray lined with a lace doily. Serbians are gracious hosts and make visitors feel very special and very welcome.

Festivals in Serbia and around the world give people a chance to celebrate their ethnic heritage. They are a time to wear traditional costumes and enjoy the music, dance, food, and other customs of a culture. Festivals give visitors to Serbia a special opportunity to learn about its traditions.

**A young girl dressed up for a Slavic festival**

### In the South—Kosovo Province

Turkish influence has been strong in Kosovo for centuries. This is especially obvious in the province's beautiful, rounded architecture. And Turkish coffee is served throughout Serbia. It is finely ground and very strong coffee that is boiled and served in small cups.

### Say Hello

When you are introduced to someone in Serbia, you shake hands and both you and the other person say your own first and last names. It's a great way to remember names.

**Men drinking Turkish coffee at a café**

Centuries ago, the Serbian culture began in the Kosovo region. Today, most of the people who live there are ethnic Albanians. Their culture is quite different from that of the Serbians. First, they are mostly Muslims, while most Serbians are Orthodox Christians. Albanians often have eight or more children. Families are tightly knit, and the man is the head of the household. Extended families, including aunts, uncles, and grandparents, often live in a group of houses surrounded by a thick stone wall or cement fence.

Though most of the younger generation wear Western-style clothing, you can still see older women wearing traditional garb that includes a head scarf, long wide pants, and a loose, long-sleeved blouse. Older Albanian men often wear small white caps. The Albanian language is widely spoken throughout Kosovo.

Older Albanian men in Kosovo often wear small white caps.

# Traditions, Faith, and Folktales

The people of Serbia follow three primary religions: Eastern Orthodox, Roman Catholic, and Islamic. Orthodoxy and Catholicism follow the teachings of Christ. Islam is a major world religion founded in Arabia and based on the teachings of Muhammad.

**A**T ONE TIME, THERE was only one Christian religion. Then, in 1054, the church powers in Rome and Constantinople disagreed. This conflict, known as the Great Schism, separated these two Christian churches.

### Orthodoxy

The Eastern Orthodox Church believes that its practices follow the original Christian faith. While there are differences between the two organizations, the root of their beliefs is the same. One difference is that Orthodox priests may marry but Roman Catholic priests may not.

Most people in Serbia are Eastern Orthodox Christians. The Orthodox religion is tied to the beginnings of the Serbian state. When Serbia was formed in the twelfth century, it was customary for the church and the state to be bound together.

**Orthodox Serbs celebrating Easter**

*Opposite:* **Consecration of the Saint Sava Church in Belgrade**

**Religions of Yugoslavia\***

| | |
|---|---|
| Eastern Orthodox | 65% |
| Islamic | 19% |
| Roman Catholic | 4% |
| Protestant | 1% |
| Other | 11% |

\*Statistics include Serbia and Montenegro.

In fact, one of the main requirements for state independence was the establishment of an independent church. The Serbian Orthodox Church was established in 1219.

Stefan Nemanja, the first king of Serbia, was crowned in 1220. His brother later achieved sainthood and carried the name Saint Sava. Though he was born to a very wealthy and powerful family, Sava chose to dedicate his life to the heavenly kingdom. He was a religious man and very well educated. He taught the Serbian people religious values and also helped educate them. Over time, people followed his teachings and the church became extremely important to the Serbian people. Saint Sava's words gave Serbs great comfort in difficult times. When the Turks conquered Serbia, they allowed the church to continue. The religion helped to unite the Serbs and keep their culture alive during the long years of Ottoman rule.

### Saint Sava

Though more than 700 years have passed since the death of Saint Sava, his teachings continue to influence Serbian people today. There are many Saint Sava churches in Serbia and throughout the world, especially in the United States and Canada. Saint Sava is celebrated as Serbia's first teacher and as patron saint of the nation. When completed, the magnificent Saint Sava Church in Belgrade will be the largest of its kind. The Orthodox priests shown here are standing beneath a portrait of Saint Sava.

## The Five Pillars of Islam

Islam was introduced to the Balkan region centuries ago by Ottoman Turks. The Islamic holy book is known as the Koran. People who follow the teachings of Islam are called Muslims.

Five duties are required of all Muslims. The first is to publicly declare their creed, which says that Allah is the one God

**Muslim men pray at a mosque in Priština.**

and Muhammad is his prophet. The second duty is five daily prayers: before sunrise, in early afternoon, in late afternoon, immediately after sunset, and before retiring. The third duty is to give money to the poor; the fourth is to fast during the month of Ramadan. The fifth duty is to make a pilgrimage to Mecca at least once, if not prevented by ill health or poverty.

Many people were forcibly converted to Islam during the Ottoman Empire's 500-year occupation of Serbia. The religion is still practiced in Serbia today, primarily in Kosovo Province.

Young women study the Koran at a mosque in Belgrade

### Holidays and Traditions

Serbians are a passionate and dramatic people, and those qualities are evident in their celebrations. Rich cultural traditions play a part in holidays, weddings, and special relationships. Serbians and other Orthodox followers throughout the world celebrate Christmas on January 7 instead of December 25. The date is different because the Orthodox follow an older calendar for their holy days.

The Serbian word for Christmas is *Božić* (bow-zich). It comes from the word *Bog*, or God, and means "Infant God." On Christmas morning in Serbia, you don't just wake up and tear into gifts. Instead, you must wait for someone to bring Christmas into your house. This "someone" is a specially selected young child or neighbor who knocks on the door to "bring in the spirit of Christ." The youngster pokes a stick into the fireplace, and the number of sparks that fly up indicates how much luck the family will have in the year ahead. The young person is given gifts in thanks for bringing the spirit of Christ into the home.

Serbian Orthodox Christmas Eve is a lovely event. The evening is called *Badnje Vece* (BUD-neyea-vech-eh). *Badnjak* means "yule log." Branches of an oak tree are brought to the church courtyard and a bonfire is lit. Neighbors, friends, and families gather around the fire as the priest blesses it and the

**Česnica bread**

church choir sings Christmas hymns. The burning of the yule log symbolizes Christ, who is said to give light in darkness and warmth against cold. After the ceremony, people get together in the church hall to chat and eat Lenten foods (no meat or dairy products). People also enjoy a special drink called a "hot toddy," which consists of heated brandy sweetened with honey.

The main foods of the Christmas feast are roast pork and a special bread called *česnica* (CHES-knee-tsa). This delicious round bread is decorated with special symbols, and a coin is baked inside. The bread is broken apart, and whoever gets the piece with the coin is said to have good luck for the next year.

## A Saint to Watch Over the Family

*Slava* means "giving thanks." In Serbian tradition, every family has a patron saint that protects them. The family honors their special saint on a day called *Krsna Slava*, or "patron saint day." These celebrations occur throughout the year and are passed down from father to son. It is a day of feasting and giving thanks. Family and friends are all invited to celebrate.

The special religious rituals for Slava day include the lighting of a Slava candle so that the light of the saint may shine through the day. A Slava *kolać* (ko-lach), a round bread, and *žito* (zhee-toe), a boiled, sweetened wheat, are also prepared. Each guest takes a small spoonful of wheat in memory of those who have passed away.

A priest comes into the house and blesses all the rooms with holy water and incense to keep out evil spirits. The family and priest gather in a circle and turn the bread around while they sing a special song. The priest blesses the bread with wine, and the father or the oldest son breaks the bread in half. Each member of the family kisses the bread while the priest says, "God is in our midst." The family member responds, "He is and always will be."

### Christmas Eve at Home

After church, everyone brings home some oak branches and bunches of straw. These are spread out in the home to symbolize the manger where Christ was born. In keeping with other dramatic traditions, the way in which the straw is placed is great fun. Children gather behind their mother and follow her as she parades around the house. She makes the sound of a hen, "cluck, cluck, cluck," and the children, pretending to be little chicks, cry "peeyoo, peeyoo, peeyoo!"

## Kumovi—An Extension of Family

Many centuries ago when Christians began to baptize children, the custom of a sponsor was introduced. That sponsor was called the godfather. In Serbian he is called *kum* (koom), and the godmother is called *kuma*. *Kumovi* (koo-moh-vee), or god-parents, are responsible for the baby if anything should happen to the parents. They also name the child.

Kumovi become valued members of the family. They are not blood relatives, but they are just as important. Kumovi are like well-respected "spiritual" family members. A Serbian expression reveals how important the kum is: *God in heaven and the kum on Earth*.

Serbians have kumovi for baptisms and for weddings. In Vojvodina, kumovi have a very honored wedding seat. An old tradition requires that no one eat a bite until after the kum or kuma of the wedding has begun to eat. And when the kumovi leave the reception, they are not allowed to walk on the ground. They walk on chairs placed from the reception hall to a waiting car, and musicians serenade them all the way.

In the villages, wedding celebrations can last several days. Guests generally stay with family and close friends. After the couple return from their honeymoon, the bride stands at the doorway of her new house. She lifts a baby boy three times and asks that her marriage be blessed with children.

**A wedding celebration**

## For the Souls of the Dearly Departed

Funerals are elaborate affairs, and many people are invited to attend the burial. At the burial site, tables are set up for a lavish meal of salads and roasted meats to honor the person who died. A similar large gathering is held after a year when the gravestone is set in the ground. In addition to inscriptions, photos are placed on gravestones.

## Folktales

Folktales are meant to teach moral values and often feature animals or people with special powers. Some stories are meant to keep children in line by telling them that a "boogie man" will get them if they don't behave. The Serbian version of the boogie man is called "Baba Roga." She is an ugly old witch who is said to take bad children away from their families if they don't listen to their mother and father.

Another popular story features a dog and a piece of meat. One day a dog was carrying a piece of delicious meat in his mouth. As he was crossing a mountain stream, he looked down and saw his own reflection. He thought the reflection was another dog with an even larger piece of meat. When he tried to grab it, he dropped his own meat and the stream carried it away. The dog tried to blame the river for stealing his food, but the river told him if he wasn't so greedy he wouldn't have lost his meat in the first place.

**A watercolor of Baba Roga by Dragan Kecman**

# Pictures, Words, and Music

Whether they are eight or eighty years old, artists use their own personal view of the world in their work. It takes skill, imagination, and courage to be an artist. Their works often cause us to have some emotional reaction—we feel sad, happy, or perhaps even angry.

"I believe everyone has a special gift that has to be given away to the world. The more of it you give, the more you discover yourself. The more of yourself that you discover, the more you want to give away. That is, I believe, the great purpose of life."

–Zoran Maširević, television and film director

SOME ART IS MEANT TO BE EXPERIENCED IN A PERSONAL WAY, like reading a book or looking at a painting. Other kinds of art can bring people together, like theater, music, and dance. But no matter when it was created, the beauty of art is timeless. We can look at objects that were made centuries ago and still appreciate the magnificence of the work.

*Opposite:* **Snacks for sale in Skadarlija, Belgrade's artists' quarter**

**A mosaic of Jesus Christ at Oplenac**

### Visual Arts

Serbia has been occupied by outsiders at times, and at other times it has been a free nation. The art of Serbia has been influenced by others, and it has also contributed to various European art movements. Among the more significant artistic developments has been sacred or religious art. Frescoes and mosaics adorn the walls, floors, and ceilings of monasteries and churches throughout Serbia.

## National Museum in Belgrade

The National Museum was founded in 1844. Its most well known collections include prehistoric ceramics, Greek and Roman jewelry, copies of medieval frescoes, Serbian icons, and many modern works by Serbian and French artists, especially the Impressionists.

The word *fresco* means "fresh" in Italian. It is a method of painting with watercolors on wet plaster. Mosaics are made of many-colored small pieces of glass, stone, ceramic, or other materials. In some of Serbia's churches, gold leaf has been used as a mosaic material.

### Painting Today

Serbia's strong artistic heritage is very much alive today. You can see both modern and historic ideas in today's paintings. They include elements of the ancient Lepenski Vir rocks, Byzantine style, religious ideas, and surrealism, or fantasy. Well-known artists who have exhibited their work around the world include the late Milan Konjović, who used bright colors and nature motifs, and Milić Stanković, whose works include oil paintings of Serbian life as well as some fine illustrations. Olja Ivanički's paintings include figurative and surrealistic images.

### A Gathering Place for Artists

Skadarlija (SKA-darl-lee-ya) was a gathering place in Belgrade for famous writers and artists at the end of the nineteenth century. A brewery at the end of Skadarska Street, which gave the neighborhood its name, led to the opening of many taverns, restaurants, and shops.

Today people of all ages meet in Skadarlija to sip coffee, browse the art galleries, eat good food, and enjoy plays and cabarets.

### Dragan Kecman

Dragan "Joyce" Kecman is among the up-and-coming artists in Serbia. He was born in the small town of Kučevo, where he now has a studio and exhibition gallery. His images appear to be gently floating in space, giving his paintings a part-reality, part-dreamlike quality. His work is collected by art lovers around the world.

## Folk Arts and Crafts

Art can be both practical and decorative. In Serbia, the applied arts include textiles, pottery, etched crystal, intricate lacework, and carved and inlaid wood. The architecture of buildings and churches can also be considered practical works of art.

**Folk textiles of Serbia**

Serbia's textiles are made from its abundant supply of wool, flax, and hemp. The handmade carpets are colorful and very durable. They are often composed with geometric patterns such as zigzags, squares, and steps. These rugs are still available today, mostly in the markets of smaller towns and villages.

One kind of folk art that originated with the Slavic people is now widely known—egg decoration. You may know it as the Easter egg. In old Serbia, natural dyes were used. Boiled onion peels turned the egg a lovely amber or pale yellow, depending on the kind of onion skin used.

## Egg Tapping

Serbian Easter includes a special ritual with Easter eggs. Children and adults tap their eggs together to see which egg is strongest. One person holds an egg in his fist with only the tip showing while another person taps it with the tip of her own egg. The winner is the one whose egg does not crack. As you might imagine, a lot of eggs get smashed.

### Literature

It is said that painting is like visual poetry, and that poetry paints pictures. Serbia has a long literary history. From the thirteenth-century epic poetry of Kosovo to modern novels, Serbians love to tell a good story. In the 1800s, two great poets were recognized beyond the borders of Serbia—Jovan Jovanović Zmaj and Djura Jakšić.

## Songs of Times Past

A *gusle* (goose-la) is a traditional one-stringed instrument.

### Grandfather and Grandson

*The Grandfather took his grandson*
*Put him on his knee,*
*And with gusle he did sing*
*Of all that used to be.*

*He sang to him of Serbian glory*
*Serbian knights of old*
*He sang to him of battles fierce*
*And suffering untold.*

*And grandfather's eye did glisten*
*As he shed a tear*
*And then his little grandson bade*
*To kiss the gusle dear.*

*The child did kiss the ancient gusle*
*Then he asked in bliss*
*"Tell me, Grand-dad, why did I*
*The gusle yonder kiss?"*

*"You know not, my little Serb*
*But we, your elders do.*
*When you grow up and think it*
*  through*
*It will all just come to you."*
    *–Jovan Jovanović Zmaj*

(Courtesy of *Little Falcons Magazine*, edited by Father Thomas Kazich, Grayslake, Ill.)

Isidora Sekulić (1877–1958) was the first woman to become a member of the Serbian Academy of Arts and Sciences. When she was fourteen years old, she was already fluent in five languages—German, French, Russian, Italian, and Serbian. She was known for her original stories and for her ability to translate difficult writings. Like many artists, she was a bit eccentric. One day while she was strolling through a park in Belgrade, an officer of King Aleksandar invited her to visit the king. She thought it over for moment, then said, "Please tell the king not to be offended, but I have no time for him at the moment." She then continued her walk through the park, perhaps thinking over a story line for her next piece of writing.

The world has recognized many excellent Serbian writers. Mihajlo Pupin, a Serbian scientist who immigrated to the United States in 1874, was also a distinguished writer. He won a Pulitzer Prize for his autobiography, *From Immigrant to Inventor*. In his book he talks about what made him curious. "Herding oxen with other village boys, I watched stars at night and thought their light was a language of God…. I didn't know how that language reached me and hoped someday that I might find out." He didn't just wonder, he found answers to his questions. Pupin became a famous professor of physics at Columbia University in New York.

Nobel Prize–winner Ivo Andrić *(second from left)* and others pose together before receiving their prizes.

Today you can see a building there that has been dedicated in his honor.

In 1961, Ivo Andrić became the first Yugoslav to receive the Nobel Prize, for his novel *Bridge over the River Drina*. Other popular authors today include Milorad Pavić and Vladimir Arsenijević, whose books have been translated into many languages.

## Stories on Screen

Films made by Serbian directors have also been exported to other countries. These films are often produced on very small budgets, especially when they are compared to multimillion-dollar Hollywood films. But the emotional power of the stories told in Serbian films can make them as moving as the most costly blockbusters.

When we talk about the history of filmmaking in Serbia, we need to do so from the point of view of Yugoslavia. Remember, there were once six republics within it, while only two remain today. The funds, talent, and production centers developed across Yugoslavia as a whole.

The first film recordings began in 1905. The filmmaker Milton Manaki started by simply shooting some scenes of ordinary life in his small town. His first full-length film, completed in 1910, told the story of the Serbian Karadjordjević Dynasty. It was a coproduction between Belgrade and Paris.

The films produced during World War I and World War II were mostly educational, tourist, and war documentary films. The film industry began to expand in 1945. At that time, the government began to pay for productions. By the 1960s, Yugoslavia's economy had improved, and the number of film productions increased along with it.

The world really began to take notice of Yugoslav filmmaking in the 1980s. The most influential director was Emir Kusturica, who was born in Sarajevo. His films were about human relationships and struggles with the government. His second film, *When Father Was Away on Business*, won first place at the Cannes Film Festival. He was the first director to openly show how fearful people were of Communism and how innocent citizens were imprisoned for no reason. He greatly influenced many directors. He often worked with musical composer Goran Bregović. That partnership proved to be successful for both

**Kusturica's American Period**

In the early 1990s, the famous director Emir Kusturica spent several years in the United States teaching filmmaking at Columbia University. During that time he shot *Arizona Dreaming*, a movie featuring Johnny Depp, Faye Dunaway, and Jerry Lewis.

of them. A number of Kusturica's films are available in the United States with English subtitles. The music of Bregović is also widely available.

Though the civil war in the 1990s cut the number of films being produced, the Serbians' creativity did not diminish. There were many types of films, including comedies, tragedies, and romances. They dealt with subjects such as love, greed, adventure, and disaster. Especially popular were films about the war. Often they showed how ordinary people were affected by the tragedy.

Perhaps more than any subject, Serbian filmmakers are masters at revealing the depth and drama of human relation-

**Film director Srdjan Dragojević**

ships. They portray emotions we have all felt. Because these films are so powerful, many viewers walk away with a new outlook on the world.

One such powerful film is *Pretty Village, Pretty Flame*, directed by Srdjan Dragojević. The film focuses on two young men who were best friends all their lives. One of them is a Serbian and the other, a Muslim. Then the 1990s civil war hits their town—a war among Serbs, Croats, and Muslims, which instantly made enemies of friends. These two young men are caught in the middle and must choose between their friendship and the politics of war. The film has been praised by critics worldwide and has attracted the attention of Hollywood agents.

Zoran Maširević is another Serbian television and film director whose stories tell us what war does to ordinary people. His film *The Border* is set on the border between Yugoslavia and Hungary and takes place in 1948. World War II has ended, but people are still angry. A young Yugoslav boy falls in love with a Hungarian girl. At first, their families refuse to let the young couple be together. But love being love, they find a way to see each other. Eventually they marry, and their union serves to pull the families together. *The Border* won numerous awards and has been shown around the world. Maširević now lives and works in Los Angeles, California.

## Actors and Screenwriters

Well-known American actors of Serbian descent include John Malkovich (near right), Karl Malden, and Lolita Davidovich (far right). Steven Tesich is a well-known screenwriter. American actors have also appeared in Yugoslav films. Brad Pitt's first starring role in a feature film was in a 1988 Yugoslav production titled *The Dark Side of the Sun*. The film was lost during the civil war in Yugoslavia and was not rediscovered until 1996.

## Music

Music is a universal language. Like other arts in Serbia, its history begins a long time ago. In the thirteenth century, wandering gusle players sang about current events. They played the gusle much as you would play a violin. The players of this instrument were called *guslari* (GOOS-la-ree). They traveled from village to village singing ballads about history and bringing news to the people.

Tamburitza orchestras play another kind of folk music on special stringed instruments similar to mandolins and banjos. The musicians, called *tamburashi* (tom-BOO-rah-she), are highly skilled and they play with energy and enthusiasm. Often, small groups of three or four players get together at a social event, and people dance and sing with the band. The festivities may last very late.

Today in Serbia, all kinds of music can be heard on the radio. What's interesting is the mix—everything from traditional folk music to rock and roll to classical—played back to back on the same station. Serbia imports a great deal of popular music from the United States and Britain, but it has its own pop stars too.

A gusle player

### Tipping Tamburashi

If someone requests a song, the musicians are tipped in an amusing way. The person places a bill on the neck of the instrument, or sticks the money onto the perspiring forehead of the musician.

Young people listen to everything from pop to rap, including Michael Jackson, Madonna, Celine Dion, and C-Block. Bands like *Bjelo Dugme* (White Button) and *Ribja Corba* (Fish Stew) are among the well-known Yugoslav rock musicians. They incorporate American rock with Serbian ethnic sounds. Their music is available on audiocassettes and compact discs, so it can be enjoyed everywhere.

## Dance

Serbia celebrates dance with formal ballet performances at the National Theater in Belgrade and folklore groups that travel around the country. *Kolos* are traditional Serbian circle dances. These dances are performed by professional troupes and by ordinary citizens, too. It's a festive and friendly way to dance. People hold hands and form a half circle. One person leads the string of people around the dance floor. Everyone dances—grandmothers, teenage boys, aunts, and neighbors.

Kolo dancing is most often seen at weddings and other special gatherings. Some dances are slow, while others are fast and require some fancy footwork as well as good aerobic conditioning. Dancing a few of the faster kolos is as good as jogging a mile or more.

Images of people dancing kolos can be seen in old frescoes. The Turks who occupied Serbia were very strict. During their rule, people were not allowed to gather just to talk, but they could socialize on special occasions. The kolo dances were a way for people to communicate. They would send messages to each other through the lyrics to the kolo music. The Turks thought people were just having fun, and they

Kolo dancing

were. But they were also spreading news.

In towns and cities today, young people dance at discos on Saturday nights. A variety of popular music is played, most of it rock-based. There are a few differences between Serbian discos and those in the United States. In Serbia, young people of all ages are allowed to enter discos. When a well-known song is played, many people sing along. And girls don't wait for boys to ask them to dance—it is totally acceptable for girls to dance together.

# At Home, at School, at Play

Families in Serbia tend to be very close. It is not unusual to find parents, their adult children, and even grandchildren living together in the same home. Even when they do not share a home, people often stay close to where they were born. Cousins, aunts, uncles, and grandparents may all live in same town, perhaps even next door to one another.

*Opposite:* **An informal soccer game**

S ERBIA'S SOCIETY, LIKE SOCIETIES IN OTHER PARTS OF THE world, is paternalistic. In a paternalistic society, a woman takes her husband's last name in marriage, and the husband is considered the head of the household. It is his responsibility

**A Serbian family at home**

to work and provide food and shelter for his family. In Serbia today, many women work outside the home too. There is an old Serbian saying that the husband is the head of the house and the woman is the foundation. In other words, it takes both husband and wife to make a successful family. Each contributes to the welfare of their home and children.

In the Serbian language, there is no direct translation for the word *cousin*. Cousins are referred to as "sisters" or "brothers." Although that may cause some confusion about family relationships, it also creates a special closeness.

## Games

Many of the games children play in Serbia are the same games children play in the United States and Canada. Young children play hide-and-seek, hopscotch, and jump rope. Video games are popular, especially in the cities, where game parlors are filled with blinking lights and sound effects. Outdoors, people play basketball and *fudbal* (food-bawl), or soccer. Soccer is very popular throughout Serbia. Most communities have leagues for children from ages five to fifteen. The basketball court and the soccer field are popular places after school hours.

## Spectator Sports

There are professional organized sports as well. Soccer, hockey, and basketball are among the most popular spectator sports. Serbians are known for their great skill in basketball. The Yugoslav team came very close to beating the U.S. team

**Pistol Pete Maravich**

A number of athletes of Yugoslavian ancestry play basketball on American teams. Among the better known is Pete Maravich, who was born in the United States to Serbian parents. He played professionally for the Atlanta Hawks and the Boston Celtics in the 1970s and 1980s. He was known as "Pistol Pete" for his speed.

Yugoslavia took home a silver medal for basketball in the 1996 Olympics.

in the 1996 Olympics. They came in second, winning the silver medal. The Serbians are also well known for their rifle-shooting skills. Women have brought home Olympic gold in that sport—Aleksandra Ivošev in 1996 and Jasna Sekarić in 1992. Handball, water polo, and volleyball are other sports at which Serbian athletes excel.

Aleksandra Ivošev shows off her gold medal.

*Opposite:* **Cafés surround Terazije Square in Belgrade.**

## Meeting Friends

Whether visiting one another for afternoon coffee or meeting later in the evening, Serbians love to socialize. After dinner on warm summer evenings, every town has a *korzo* (KOHR-zo). The main street is closed to traffic, and people slowly stroll the street, greeting neighbors and friends. Both children and adults come out for korzo. It is an excellent way for people to stay in touch.

The main street is usually lined with cafés, or *kafanas* (ka-FUN-ahs). Serbians love their cafés. Now that the government allows people to own private businesses, there are cafés on almost every corner. People stop for a Turkish coffee or perhaps a *sok* (sawk), a refreshing fruit drink.

### Greetings

It is not unusual for friends and family to kiss each other on the cheek when they see each other. Men kiss men, and women kiss women. Three kisses in all—first one cheek, then the other, then the first cheek again. The custom is similar to shaking hands but is a much warmer greeting.

Primary school students in a classroom

## Education

Schools are free and very demanding. Serbian students who have come to the United States to study have often remarked how much easier it is for them to get high marks in U.S. schools. In Serbia, school is mandatory up to age sixteen.

After the first eight years of school, most children attend secondary schools (*sredjna skola*), where they select a skilled vocation or a field for advanced education. Secondary schools last three or four years depending on the vocation. Students can

### Serbian National Holidays

| | |
|---|---|
| New Year | January 1 |
| International Labor Day | May 1 |
| Day of Uprising in Serbia | July 7 |
| Republic Day | November 29 |

study anything from electronics to medicine. After secondary school, they have enough knowledge and skills to get a job. They can also go to a university to continue their studies in their chosen field. About one-third of pupils attend *gimnazija*, which provide them with a broad academic education. Requirements in gimnazija include Latin, philosophy, art, and biology. After these studies, students go on to university. The main difference between srednja skola and gimnazija is that srednja skola train students to enter the work force, while gimnazija prepares them for intensive university study. Studies at a university last four to six years depending on the field of study.

**Ballet students practice at the barre.**

An informal poll in 1998 asked Belgrade secondary students at the Ivo Andrić School this question: "What would you like others your age to know about Serbia?" Here are a few of their responses:

"We are like teenagers everywhere, come visit us."

"Though small, Serbia has a big heart and soul."

"I would like to sing you a song and invite you to visit my beautiful country."

"No matter where you are from, Serbia will accept you with open arms."

## At Home

Most Serbian homes are smaller than those in the United States and Canada. Children often share a bedroom. Kitchens are for food preparation only, and meals are eaten in a dining room.

Most city dwellings have central heat today. In the smaller towns, people still use coal or woodstoves to heat their homes. The scent of wood and coal fills the air. Though stoves heat homes fairly well, electrical heaters are fast replacing them because they are much more convenient. There's no wood to chop and no messy black coal to store.

Electricity is commonly available. In fact, Serbia and Romania built one of Europe's largest hydroelectric stations,

### Nikola Tesla (1856–1943)

Nikola Tesla immigrated to the United States after completing his science studies in Europe. He worked for a short time with Thomas Edison, who called Tesla "a poet of science." The two eventually became rivals. Tesla's idea of connecting alternating current (AC) to a motor eventually led to the development of power stations in the United States and around the world. Tesla received 112 U.S. patents for his discoveries. A statue honoring him was erected at Goat Island power station, Niagara Falls.

on the Danube River near the Lepenski Vir area. The electricity generated there flows throughout Yugoslavia. People use electricity to power everything from blow-dryers to telephone-answering machines to computers. A famous Serbian engineer and inventor by the name of Nikola Tesla contributed greatly to the evolution of the electrical current we all use today.

## Food

The tasty food served throughout Serbia focuses on the basic food groups: vegetables, fruits, meats, dairy, and breads. Though rice and pasta are available, they are not eaten in great abundance. Breakfast often includes eggs, meat, and bread, and sometimes yogurt and cheese. *Kajmak* (KAY-mak) is a Serbian specialty. It tastes like a blend of butter and cream cheese. People use kajmak for baking or as a spread for bread.

The main meal of the day is eaten in the afternoon, generally about 3:00 P.M. Schools are out, and so are many businesses. The workday is generally from 8:00 A.M. to 2:00 P.M. with no lunch break, and people often work a half-day on Saturdays as well. What do people eat for lunch? Usually quite a bit! Roasted meats, stews, cheeses, and freshly baked bread are a typical afternoon meal. Of course, after such a hearty meal, many people take a brief nap. Dinner is usually a light meal, eaten about eight o'clock in the evening.

To eat in Serbia in the summertime is a delicious experience. Lots of locally grown fruits and vegetables are available throughout the growing season. There are cherry trees and many varieties of plums, pears, and peaches. You'll also see small home gardens with tomatoes, green onions, garlic, and herbs.

**Peppers for sale at a market**

**Everyone loves *palačinke*!**

Peppers are used in many dishes—peppers stuffed with special meats and then baked, peppers pickled in a jar, or simply peppers sliced into a salad of tomatoes and onions. In a few national specialties you can taste a bit of Serbia in every bite. *Proja* is a corn bread with kajmak cheese and ham, and *gibanica* is crispy, paper-thin dough layered with cheese and egg. Serbia's spiced sausages are delicious and so are *sarma*—meat-stuffed cabbage leaves—and *djuveć*, a tomato-based vegetable stew. Desserts include dry *pita* (strudel) with walnuts, apples, or sour cherry, and *palačinke* (crepes).

## Beating the Summer Heat

In summer, people stay cool in the shade. Grapevines, which produce lots of green leaves, are often draped over wooden frames in town and country. Families place picnic tables under this cool green canopy. Many people barbecue and enjoy dining outside in the summer.

### How to Make a Palačinka

A *palačinka* (pah-lah-CHEEN-ka) is a crepe, basically a thin pancake, and very easy to make. This recipe makes 4 or 5 palačinke (*palačinke* is the plural).

   1 egg
   1 cup milk
   1 cup flour
   cooking oil
   favorite jam
   powdered sugar
   frying pan a bit smaller than a dinner plate

Add one egg to a cup of milk and beat well. Then add a cup of flour and blend. The mixture should be thinner than a mixture for pancakes. Heat a tablespoon of oil in a frying pan until it begins to crackle. Pour about 1/4 cup of the mixture into the pan and spread it around so that it is thin. When the color changes to a deeper yellow and the mixture looks firm, flip it with a spatula. It will fry quickly on the second side. Flip the palačinka onto a plate. Fry the rest of the batter the same way, adding oil each time if needed. Once the palačinka has cooled, spread it with a tablespoon of your favorite jam. Fold it in half lengthwise, then fold it across. Sprinkle it with a little powdered sugar and enjoy!

## Ćevapčići

*Ćevapčići* (chee-VAHP-chee-chee) are small sausages made of pork, lamb, beef, and special spices. They are grilled outdoors, and you can smell the sweet scent for blocks. Ćevapčići are eaten with fresh bread and diced white onions throughout Serbia.

# Timeline

c. 2500 B.C.  Egyptians build the Pyramids and Sphinx in Giza.

563 B.C.  Buddha is born in India.

## Serbian History

A.D. 313  The Roman emperor Constantine recognizes Christianity.

610  The prophet Muhammad begins preaching a new religion called Islam.

1054  The Eastern (Orthodox) and Western (Roman) Churches break apart.

1066  William the Conqueror defeats the English in the Battle of Hastings.

1095  Pope Urban II proclaims the First Crusade.

Nemanja Dynasty begins.  1159

Saint Sava establishes the Serbian Orthodox Church.  1219

Stefan Nemanja is crowned as Serbia's first king.  1220

1215  King John seals the Magna Carta.

1300s  The Renaissance begins in Italy.

Battle of Kosovo  1389

Ottoman Empire rules Serbia.  1389–1815

1347  The Black Death sweeps through Europe.

1453  Ottoman Turks capture Constantinople, conquering the Byzantine Empire.

1492  Columbus arrives in North America.

1500s  The Reformation leads to the birth of Protestantism.

## Serbian History

| | |
|---|---|
| Serbian peasant George Petrović leads uprising against the Turks. | **1804** |
| Serbian leader Miloš Obrenović leads second revolt. | **1815** |
| Serbia regains independence following the Ottoman Empire's defeat by Russia and Serbia. | **1878** |
| During Balkan Wars, Serbia and other Balkan countries gain control of most Ottoman Empire possessions in Europe. | **1912** |
| Austria declares war on Serbia, starting World War I (1914–1918). | **1914** |
| Kingdom of the Serbs, Croats, and Slovenes is formed. | **1918** |
| The kingdom is renamed Yugoslavia. | **1929** |
| Serbia becomes one of the republics of the Socialist Federal Republic of Yugoslavia. | **1945** |
| Slobodan Milošević, a Serbian nationalist, becomes president of Serbia. | **1989** |
| Serbia dissolves Kosovo's parliament and ends Communist Party monopoly of power. | **1990** |
| Croatia and Slovenia declare their independence from Yugoslavia. | **1991** |
| Federal Republic of Yugoslavia is formed as self-proclaimed successor to the Socialist Federal Republic of Yugoslavia. | **1992** |
| Milošević nullifies election results when his opposition wins. Protests and demonstrations follow. | **1996** |
| Milošević is elected president of the new Yugoslavia. | **1997** |

## World History

| | |
|---|---|
| **1776** | The Declaration of Independence is signed. |
| **1789** | The French Revolution begins. |
| **1865** | The American Civil War ends. |
| **1914** | World War I breaks out. |
| **1917** | The Bolshevik Revolution brings Communism to Russia. |
| **1929** | Worldwide economic depression begins. |
| **1939** | World War II begins, following the German invasion of Poland. |
| **1957** | The Vietnam War starts. |
| **1989** | The Berlin Wall is torn down, as Communism crumbles in Eastern Europe. |
| **1996** | Bill Clinton re-elected U.S. president. |

# Fast Facts

**Official name:** Serbia

**Capital:** Belgrade

**Official language:** Serbian

Serbian flag

Slobodan Milošević

| | |
|---|---|
| **Official religion:** | Eastern Orthodox Church |
| **Year of founding:** | Late 1100s |
| **Founder:** | Stefan Nemanja |
| **Government:** | Republic |
| **Chief of state:** | President |
| **Head of government:** | Prime minister |
| **Area:** | 34,115 square miles (88,385 sq km) (slightly larger than Maine) |
| **Coordinates of geographic center:** | 44° 00' N, 21° 00' E |
| **Bordering countries:** | Montenegro, Bosnia and Herzegovina, Croatia, Hungary, Romania, Bulgaria, Macedonia, Albania |
| **Highest elevation:** | Daravica, 8,716 feet (2,656 m) |
| **Average temperatures:** | 70°F (21°C) in July; 32°F (0°C) in January |
| **Average annual rainfall:** | 25–35 inches (64–89 cm) |
| **National population (1997 est.):** | 10,543,641 |

**Population of largest cities in Serbia (1991):**

| | |
|---|---|
| Belgrade | 1,602,226 |
| Novi Sad | 179,626 |
| Niš | 175,391 |
| Kragujevac | 147,305 |
| Priština | 108,083 |
| Subotica | 100,386 |

| Famous landmarks: | **Golubac Fortress** (Iron Gate Gorge) |
| --- | --- |
| | **Kalemegdan Fortress** (Belgrade) |
| | **Lepenski Vir** archeaeological site (Djerdap National Park) |
| | **Museum of Modern Art** (Belgrade) |
| | **National Museum** (Belgrade) |
| | **Turkish Baths and Sinan-pasha's mosque** (Prizren) |

Currency

**Historic monasteries and churches** are found all over Serbia, including Gracanica (Priština), Krušedol and Hopovo (Fruška Gora), the Patriarchate of Peć, Studenica, and Zicak)

**National parks:** Djerdap, Fruška Gora, Kopaonik, Sara, Tara

| Industry: | Food, textile, and metal processing; automobiles and agricultural machinery; household appliances; petroleum products; pharmaceuticals |
| --- | --- |
| Currency: | One Yugoslav New Dinar (YD) contains 100 paras. In 1998 the exchange rate was YD10.83 = $U.S.1 |
| Weights and measures: | Metric system |
| Literacy rate (1991 est.): | Total population, 93%; males, 97.2%, females, 88.9% |

| Famous Serbians: | Ivo Andrić<br>*Writer* | (1892–1975) |
| --- | --- | --- |
| | Stefan Dušan<br>*King* | (1308–1388) |
| | Mileva Marić Einstein<br>*Scientist; first wife of Albert Einstein* | (1875–1948) |
| | Draža Mihajlović<br>*Soldier, resistance leader* | (1893–1946) |

Miloš Obrenović

| | |
|---|---|
| Slobodan Milošević<br>*President* | (1941–   ) |
| Stefan Nemanja<br>*Grand župan* | (d. 1200) |
| Stefan II Nemanja<br>*King* | (d. 1228) |
| Miloš Obrenović<br>*Prince* | (1780–1860) |
| Mihajlo (Michael) Pupin<br>*Scientist, writer* | (1858–1935) |
| Saint Sava<br>*Religious leader* | (c. 1176–c. 1236) |
| Isidora Sekulić<br>*Intellectual/writer* | (1877–1958) |
| Nikola Tesla<br>*Electrical engineer, inventor* | (1856–1943) |

**Common Serbian words and phrases:**

| | |
|---|---|
| *zdavo* | hello |
| *da* | yes |
| *ne* | no |
| *hvala* | thank you |
| *Razumem* | I understand |
| *Ne razumem* | I do not understand |

# To Find Out More

## Nonfiction

▶ Hunt, Inez, and Wanetta Draper. *Lightning in His Hand: Life Story of Nikola Tesla*. Thousand Oaks, Calif.: Sage Books, 1964.

▶ Kisslinger, Jerome. *The Serbian Americans*. New York: Chelsea House, 1990.

▶ *Little Falcons Magazine*. Edited by Father Thomas Kazich, published by the Serbian Orthodox Church, Grayslake, IL 60030.

▶ Pupin, Michael. *From Immigrant to Inventor*. 1924. Reprint, edited by I. Bernard Cohen. North Stratford, NH: Ayer, 1980.

▶ *Serb World USA Magazine*. Edited by Mary Nicklanovich Hart. Serb World USA, 415 E Mabel St., Tucson, AZ 85705

## Websites

▶ **www.yugoslavia.com**
http://www.yugoslavia.com
*An overview of Yugoslavian culture, news, and history*

▶ **National Tourism Organization of Serbia**
http://www.serbia-info.com/ntos
*Information on natural and cultural tourist attractions in Serbia*

▶ **Ministry for Liaisons with Serbs outside Serbia**

http://www.srbisvet.org.yu/www/esrbijat.html

*A well-illustrated overview of Serbia*

▶ **CIA World Factbook**

http://www.odci.gov/cia/publications/pubs.html

*An overview of the geography, government, and economy of Yugoslavia*

## Organizations and Embassies

▶ **Yugoslavian Embassy**
2410 California Street NW
Washington, DC 20008
(202) 462-6566

# Index

Page numbers in *italics* indicate illustrations.

# Meet the Author

JoAnn Milivojevic is a freelance writer and speaker who loves to travel and explore. During her youth, she traveled to Serbia several times and became fluent in the language. To research this book, she returned to Serbia in spring 1998. She traveled from north to south to meet with people and to photograph life and landscapes. She interviewed high school students, scholars, farmers, artists, family members, and many other people. They all helped her discover the essence of Serbia—its traditions, its talent, and its hardships. Her research also included reading many books written by both Serbians and non-Serbians alike.

JoAnn has also written and lectured about the Caribbean. Her travel stories have appeared in magazines and newspapers nationwide, Fodor's Caribbean guidebook series, and a children's book on Puerto Rico. This is her first book for Children's Press.

JoAnn earned her B.A. in telecommunications from Indiana University and continued her education by pursuing a master's degree in creative writing. In 1980, she began her career in broadcasting by working in radio. She eventually worked for several television stations as a writer/producer.

Today, she continues to produce select video projects and to write books, magazine articles, and interactive multimedia scripts for corporations. She is also at work on fiction projects.

Her dog, Tolstoy, is her inspiration and constantly reminds her that roaming the great outdoors is as important to writing as tapping away on the keyboard.

# Photo Credits